Praise for Stretch – Leading Beyond Boundaries

A key question for those who want to help others is how to get new ideas across in a fun, interesting way which allows them to be painlessly absorbed. Brook and Brewerton achieve just this by drawing on the inherent attraction of our brain to a good story. This book is immensely readable, packed with great information in an easy to digest style. I think managers, leaders and trainers alike will love this book, and I highly recommend it for those interested in developing their 'leadership edge'.

Sarah Lewis, Psychologist,
Author and Appreciative Inquiry Consultant

Stretch is written as a fable, but it is based on reality. It describes the journey of a leader who moves from one worldview to another. Many people have had such epiphanies, but few have had the tools to move from enlightenment to execution to excellence. This book provides a practical toolkit for making that happen and achieving on-going success.

Mike Pegg, Author and Founder, The Strengths Foundation

Brook and Brewerton offer four habits to stretch yourself beyond being an ordinary Joe at work. Stretch along with Joe on the path of possibility with shared vision, sparked engagement, skilled execution and sustained progress. Warning: This book may be habit forming and work may never be so limiting again.

David Zinger, Founder and Host of the 5000 member
Employee Engagement Network

An inspiring book based upon an excellent, true-to-life case study that makes the strength coaching process come alive. It clearly identifies how strength-based leadership and coaching are needed on executive levels to deal with today's business complexity and create effective management teams. An inspiring approach that gets the best out of your teams and individuals.

Rudi Plettinx, Vice President and Managing Director, Center
for Creative Leadership Europe, Middle East and Africa

Stretch

Leading Beyond Boundaries

James Brook and Dr Paul Brewerton

Matador
9 Priory Business Park
Kibworth Beauchamp
Leicestershire LE8 0RX, UK
Tel: (+44) 116 279 2299
Fax: (+44) 116 279 2277
Email: books@troubador.co.uk
Web: www.troubador.co.uk/matador

ISBN 978 1780884 189

British Library Cataloguing in Publication Data.
A catalogue record for this book is available from the British Library.

Typeset in Verdana by Troubador Publishing Ltd

Matador is an imprint of Troubador Publishing Ltd

Acknowledgements

This book has been over 18 months in the making and would not be finished without the contribution, inspiration and support of a large number of people.

Our deepest gratitude goes out to to Nicki Hayes, who helped us transform this work from its rough early form to the polished story you are about to read. She demonstrated diligence and good humour throughout, exercising tremendous flexibility, patience and creativity in responding to our demanding expectations.

We also want to express special thanks to several other people who contributed to the book in a variety of ways: to Steph Tranter for her detailed and superb comments on virtually all aspects of the manuscript; to Gail MacIndoe for her early input into shaping some of the concepts and ideas in the book; to Tania Gonzalez for her efficient support coordinating the production and marketing of the book; and to Karena Gomez, Josh Dykstra, Aidan Tod, Alex Carr, Danielle Cunningham-Dateling, Mike Miller and Mike Pegg for their excellent comments and feedback during the final stages of writing.

Finally, a special note of thanks goes to our families (particularly Li and Ana, our partners) for giving up time with us over the weekends, evenings and holidays, to help us complete this manuscript and for continuing to support us through every step of our journey to translate our dreams into reality. Paul would also like to thank his Mum for giving him all the strength and love in the world.

Contents

Foreword

With the London Olympic and Paralympic Games now behind us, it is vital to take stock of the leadership lessons we can draw from this unforgettable celebration of sport and humanity. Although there are of course many differences between elite sports and business leadership, there are also important parallels I see from which we can draw valuable inspiration to help navigate through today's increasingly turbulent and competitive business environment.

Just like top performing athletes, effective business leaders have very different characters and strengths. They spend time analysing their strengths and natural abilities and find a place where they can shine. For business leaders, this also means using their strengths to free up and optimise the collective talents and abilities of followers in pursuit of a compelling vision.

However, the truly outstanding leaders don't stop there. Through hard work, dedication and continuous stretch of themselves, others and the organisation, they ensure they are always looking for ways to improve and take advantage of new opportunities. Like an Olympic gold medal athlete, they don't rest on their laurels when they achieve success. They look for the next challenge and work hard to move beyond their comfort zone, inspiring others to do the same. Olympians know that in their pursuit of gold, it is unlikely they will be enjoying what they do all the time. They engage in training routines that sometimes sap their energy and can't be delegated to others. They must also learn to tackle their weaker areas through hard work and by drawing on their strengths and those of others, including their coach, colleagues and team-mates. In business, it is no different. Effective leaders remain mindful of their strengths to boost their confidence, resourcefulness and energy to overcome performance blockers. They tap into the talents of those around them, using their strengths to compensate for any areas of weakness.

I would recommend this book as it is one of the few I have read that focuses on strengths-building and provides practical guidance to help leaders wanting to achieve sustainable success. *Stretch-Leading Beyond Boundaries* achieves this through a straightforward, accessible road-map to help leaders discover their unique leadership edge, develop productive habits and achieve peak performance. Through understanding and practising the habits in this book, leaders can bring the best of themselves to their roles, inspiring passion, innovation and engagement in those they lead.

Kriss Akabusi, MBE, FPSA.
Soldier, Olympic Athlete, Television Presenter and
Professional Speaker

Introduction

There are a myriad of different leadership models and approaches, many of which are highly prescriptive about the type of personality and qualities you need in order to be an effective leader. For example, qualities like charisma, persuasiveness, emotional intelligence and courage are often highlighted as essential qualities for leadership effectiveness and success.

However, recent research shows that successful leaders have very different personalities and qualities that they draw on in achieving their results. What they do have in common though, is a true understanding of and ability to leverage their 'Leadership Edge' (their unique strengths, abilities and skills) to influence and inspire others to achieve extraordinary results.

Effective leadership is also about Positive Stretch – stretching yourself and your team to push the boundaries and achieve in the upper range of your collective strengths and capabilities. This is particularly relevant in today's uncertain and competitive environment and markets, where organisations (private, public and voluntary) are all being challenged to do more with less, to work smarter and optimise the discretionary effort, ideas and morale of their workforce.

Our experience and the latest research show that the most effective leaders are masters at the art and science of stretch. They never stand still and they follow the four Stretch Leadership™ Habits. They establish a clear 'picture of success' for themselves and their organisation, *Sharing Vision*. They break the shared vision down into manageable stretch goals, *Sparking Engagement* with their team. They *Skilfully Execute* every step of the way, celebrating success and *Sustaining Progress* and positive energy throughout. In short, they push the boundaries of thinking and possibility, looking for new and innovative ways of doing things to achieve the organisation's goals, while at the same time advancing their own career.

Style of the Book

This book is written as a fable. It follows the journey of a leader with a deficit (or weakness-oriented) mindset gaining insight and experience about how to lead more effectively through stretching and optimising his own strengths, as well as the strengths of the workforce, to achieve outstanding results.

This book is intended to be a practical and accessible work of fiction, rather than an academic text. We wanted to ensure that the powerful concepts, principles and techniques we work with everyday were brought to life in a relevant and engaging way that could be embraced by as wide an audience as possible.

Although based on actual research and experiences from our own work and coaching, the characters and organisation described in the book aren't intended to reflect any specific person or organisation. Whilst the organisation in the book is a for-profit company, it could equally have been a public or voluntary sector organisation. The principles and concepts apply just as well regardless of the purpose, size, or nature of organisation, as we have experienced over the past 20 years through extensive research and leadership development experience.

Chapter 1

The Edge

**In which Joe comes to terms with his predicament
and challenges his beliefs about leadership...**

**"Look. You see? The Cliffs of Insanity!
Hurry up, move the thing, and that other thing.
MOVE IT..."
William Goldman, *The Princess Bride.*

Joe hangs up the phone on Kelly, his new boss, and walks slowly to his office window. Gazing thoughtfully across the park, he focuses on the wilting flowers in the hanging baskets, the product of a hot, dry summer. Wondering why the park wardens have not watered them, he smiles wryly, realising what his estranged wife would say, if only she were there:

"You're only worrying about the park wardens Joe, because it's easier than worrying about your own problems..."

In that second, he feels the full weight of his predicament for the first time.

As the recently appointed European head of Tiger Online Recruitment, Joe faces many challenges. The phone call he has just finished confirms this. His attention is momentarily drawn to a mother laughing as her two small children chase pigeons across the park. Wincing, he remembers his personal situation too, a situation he prefers not to think about.

'My life,' thinks Joe, 'is spinning out of control...'

Turning back to his desk, Joe forces himself to focus on his professional challenges. Front of mind is the firm's current performance. Sales are 25% behind target and several major accounts have not renewed their contracts in recent months.

Kelly had just called him from Seattle, wanting to go through all the numbers in detail to determine how to salvage the year's performance. She had sounded even more agitated than usual, particularly since sales in the US and Asia Pacific had been hit badly by the sluggish economy too.

'What if these poor sales numbers are symptomatic of deeper, more malignant problems?' ponders Joe, as he looks out of the glass partitioning between his suite and the open plan office. Thinking about his leadership team, he counts all the ways in which their performance and behaviour fail to meet his expectations.

'Relationships between individuals are poor; there's a growing mistrust and some pretty unhealthy politicking going on out there; Robert's resignation hasn't helped either,' he assesses, clinically.

Robert, Tiger's former finance director, was Joe's top performer. He had applied for Joe's job. He didn't get it. He had however, gone on to get the position as CEO for Tiger's major competitor and Joe's former employer, Dragon Recruitment.

Spinning his chair towards the window, Joe stares out at the drought trodden landscape, wondering where to start. Suddenly he remembers meeting a guy on the plane on a return trip from Seattle two weeks ago. He was a 'strengths coach'. Joe had heard of business coaches, he'd even read a few books on business coaching, never though, had he heard of a strengths coach. Being curious by nature, Joe had spent some time getting to know this person, Richard, who had given him a business card when they parted at Heathrow.

Joe remembers their conversation about the 'deficit-based' belief system most people inherit from their childhood. Richard had explained that his job was to help leaders become more effective through focussing on strengths to achieve breakthrough thinking and overcome challenges. At the time, Joe had been too embarrassed to admit that he was caught in the type of destructive energy sapping routines Richard had described as typical of a deficit-based belief system, a way of thinking that he had referred to as 'the Path of Limitation'. Thinking about it now though, he knew he'd had enough. He was tired of feeling trapped. It was time to find a way out and Richard's route had sounded pretty appealing.

Mulling over what Richard had shared with him on the plane, Joe gazes into the distance. Richard had been head of sales for one of the UK's largest advertising firms before a horrific motorbike accident on the way to his girlfriend's house had left him paralysed. An ambitious man, Richard had struggled to come to terms with this sudden and unexpected turn of events. Following six months away from work and a great deal of soul searching, Richard had decided to become an executive coach. Sharing his learning, experiences and relationship strengths with others, helping them to succeed, was the clear choice for him moving forward, he had said.

'What a tragic end to such a promising career. How on earth does he keep so positive?" ponders Joe, as he reaches for his wallet to find Richard's card.

A few seconds later, he has it. Picking up the phone, he makes the call...

The day before his meeting with Richard, Joe has his regular team meeting with Tiger's European Regional Executive Team (TERET). As well as himself, the team comprises five members: Sally, the sales and marketing director; Mark, the operations director; Raj, the technical director; Gwen, the human resources director; and Phil, the new finance director (who is fast becoming Joe's right hand man).

The meeting starts well, but within half an hour the usual petty infighting kicks off. Mark and Raj have never hit it off and this time their argument about a planned rebrand of the site is getting very personal.

"If you and your team can't get the site rebrand done by January, we should go outside to a third party web design agency, as they won't take holidays all the time, like you guys do!" Mark protests. "Besides, rebranding our web site should be a marketing project, not a technical project," adds Mark, looking hopefully at Sally, expecting her support. "I'm getting sick and tired of your constant criticism, Mark," retorts Raj, petulantly. "You know nothing about web design, yet you are always criticising what we are doing. We know what we are doing and want to do a proper job, not a half-baked one. That's why we are taking our time."

Exhausted, Joe ends the meeting, feeling utterly dejected. Yet again, his thoughts turn to his wife, Lynette. Lynette had recently left him. She had filed for divorce, citing his long work hours as one of the reasons. Joe had known that the relationship was becoming increasingly strained by his ambition and excessive working hours, but had never ever imagined that Lynette would leave, taking their two young children, Harry and Amelia, with her.

Ten minutes into his meeting with Richard, Joe feels somewhat relieved. His fear of being subjected to psychoanalysis is receding. Richard appears to be more interested in what's going on in the business than what's going on in Joe's head. Going into great detail to describe how the strengths coaching process and the Stretch Leadership™ Model work, Richard skilfully navigates Joe to a position of such comfort that, before Joe knows it, he is enjoying exploring in depth the strengths, weaknesses, opportunities and threats that Tiger faces.

"I can already see how strengths coaching is going to make an enormous impact here Joe. I sense you need quick results so I recommend we enter a coaching contract where we meet every two weeks over a six-month period. Let me explain a little more about what this would involve and what the outcomes will be," explains Richard, pulling up a slide depicting the Stretch Leadership™ Model.

Stretch Leadership™ Model

"During these sessions we will explore this proven approach to help leaders stretch their strengths to achieve positive outcomes in terms *Purpose* (a clear, compelling sense of direction and meaning), *Passion* (releasing the full energy and strengths of employees) *Process* (operational efficiency and follow-through) and *Performance* (delivering results including improved productivity and profit)." Richard hovers his cursor over the central circle.

"We will start by getting a better understanding of what you bring to this leadership role and how you can combine your core strengths, values, aspirations and abilities to move beyond boundaries – perceived or real – and give yourself what we refer to as your 'Leadership Edge'.

"We will then explore these four Stretch Leadership™ Habits:

Sharing Vision; *Sparking Engagement*; *Skilfully Executing*; and *Sustaining Success*. To help you adopt these habits, we'll look at some specific behavioural changes you may need to practise for a while until they become second nature.

"By the end of the final session, stretching your strengths – and those of your team – will have enabled you to lead your business to achieve the goals we agree on in the next few weeks, and to sustain this success beyond the coaching period," he continues.

"Think of it like a continuous journey – an expedition. The first step is to clarify and clearly communicate your aspirations, both for yourself and for this organisation (where you want to go).

"The second step is to ensure everyone is aware of where it is you want to go and how you can harness your personal, team and organisational strengths to get there (what you need to pack).

"The third step is to take action, practising your learning (selecting the best route and starting out on the journey).

"The fourth step is to become agile in stretching, and sometimes moderating, your personal, team and organisational strengths across different situations (ensuring you adapt your route when conditions change to minimise risks and get to your destination in the best way possible).

"The fifth step is to recognise the successes you have met along the path, celebrating your achievements in terms of purpose, passion, process and performance (comparable to taking time to enjoy and learn from your success when you get there, I guess).

"It's a five step journey that allows you to grow gradually and sustainably. You move from aspirations to awareness, to action, to agility, to achievement.

"It is a never ending journey though Joe, because this naturally brings you right back to the beginning, reflecting and setting new aspirations for the next expedition."

Richard looks up at Joe, as if trying to gauge whether to continue. Seeing that Joe is open to more learning, Richard decides to reveal another slide on his screen, entitled The Path of Possibility™.

The Path of Possibility™

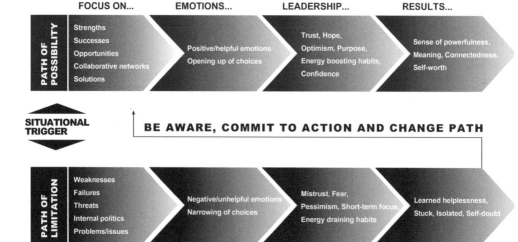

"The question is Joe, do you want to choose the Path of Limitation™, which leads to a culture of learned helplessness with individuals feeling stuck, isolated and full of self doubt and targets being missed? Or, would you prefer the Path of Possibility™, leading to a sense of positive power, with a culture where individuals feel like they are deriving meaning from their work, like they are connected to the business's success, and to each other, and where targets are always met?"

In their previous conversation, Joe had openly shared details about his recent experiences in this new position and the various issues threatening to derail him. Richard now references back to them, quickly compartmentalising them into the four different types of outcome depicted on his first slide. Joe likes that. Being able to order his perceived problems in this way somehow makes them feel more manageable. Taking the Path of Possibility™ just described to him though, sounds a little too optimistic, considering the internal weaknesses and external threats he is facing.

"Thing is Richard, I really don't know if I can. I'm not like you," states Joe, after a long pause. "I mean, how do you do it? How do you stay on the Path of Possibility™?"

"Ah. Well it is about conscious choice Joe. I've trained myself and I act very deliberately to get back onto the top path when I feel myself slipping onto the Path of Limitation™, as we all do from time to time. With good self-awareness, self-discipline and lots of practice, you too can spend more time on this positive path. I'm not saying it will be easy. It will take a lot of conscious effort, but you can train your brain to walk this path. Anyone can," Richard replies looking directly at Joe.

"First you need the willingness to change and challenge your beliefs. Once you're aware of the beliefs that you hold that are limiting you, it takes conscious effort and deep practice to re-programme them. I started by recognising my automatic reactions to situational triggers and consciously trying to replace the non-productive reactions or habits with more productive ones. For example, after I first had the accident, when people asked me what I was going to do next I'd automatically change the subject because I didn't know the answer. I didn't know the answer because, on the one hand, I still wanted to be making big money winning massive advertising contracts and on the other, I wanted something different, something more in line with my core beliefs and strengths. Deep down I knew the accident had shifted my priorities and given me an opportunity to change my career, but I was too limited by feelings of frustration, inadequacy and self-pity to make it happen."

"I eventually realised that reacting in this way was crippling me, mentally. I couldn't choose 'not to be impaired physically' but I could choose 'not to be impaired mentally'.

I chose to control the controllables and started practising to respond differently, at first with 'I'm not sure,' then with 'I want to help others,' and ultimately with 'I want to help others succeed by sharing my learning and successes'. It's what some people call realistic optimism. People who knew me before the accident know it's 'learned' realistic optimism!

"Your brain, Joe, is designed to be efficient. Everyone's is. So when your brain is under pressure, it will fall back into habits it learned early in life. Most of us have some unhealthy habits we learned early in life. They put us on the Path of Limitation™. We can only get off this path with a lot of self awareness, hard work and deliberate practice," Richard is still looking directly at Joe.

"And I know what your next question is going to be Joe," he smiles, his gaze losing its intensity.

"You do?" responds Joe, intrigued.

"Yup. You want to know if this is the right path for this organisation and I can tell you that it was *made* for this organisation. When you live in an uncertain and volatile environment, you need to create a strong culture of learning, empowerment and personal accountability. It is the only way to remain agile. Normal management rules based on logical analysis and problem solving are not enough. Exploration, experimentation and collaborative working need to be encouraged. The Path of Possibility™ does just that."

Joe just looks at Richard as if he is an unfinished puzzle. Richard is familiar with this response and knows exactly what to do next. He guides the conversation back to Joe's expectations of the coaching, bringing the first slide back onto the screen.

Stretch Leadership™ Model

"So, where's the Path of Possibility™ going to lead you Joe? What would you like the outcomes of our coaching sessions to be?" he inquires.

Joe thinks they are obvious.

"Improved results in these areas of course," he states, bluntly, pointing at the 'Purpose', 'Passion', 'Process' and 'Performance' outcomes.

"So, in order to achieve these outcomes, what areas of your current leadership style do you think we need to explore?" probes Richard.

Joe's thoughts turn immediately to his weaknesses. "Well,

that's easy. I've never been particularly collaborative or democratic in the way I work, which makes me poor at building a strong team. I'm fairly fixed in my views. I tend to judge people really quickly and will close the book on them without thinking twice if my first impressions are not favourable. I'm rarely open to persuasion and prior to this conversation, it had never actually occurred to me to look for ways to help others develop."

Richard listens attentively, making a few notes as Joe continues to talk about his weaknesses. Then, just as Joe begins to feel drained, Richard suggests, "Joe, why don't we spend some time reflecting on your successes and achievements in your 15 year career?"

Joe is surprised. He feels embarrassed 'boasting' about successes, especially in the light of all his problems. It just feels wrong. Richard raises an eyebrow encouragingly and smiles. Before Joe realises what is happening, he is recalling events and milestones in his career where he felt that he had triumphed.

"Winning the UK contract with that major oil company in my first role as a recruiter was a major turning point. It really accelerated my career. Getting headhunted by another oil company and going in-house for a while was massively rewarding too. It gave me real insights into the internal culture of large corporations.

"Then there are particular individuals that stick in my mind, for whom I found the perfect roles. I always get massive kicks out of that. I'm still in touch with some of them: Diana, who successfully moved from a CFO to a CEO role and

Ahmed, who moved through the ranks to head of HR for the oil company I was talking about, to setting up his own recruitment business, spring to mind. There are quite a lot of people now I think about it. Getting this role was a high point too, believe it or not. At the time, it felt like winning a Gold Medal!" Joe reflects.

Richard decides that this is a good point to ask: "How does it feel talking about your successes Joe?"

Joe replies: "Remarkably energising actually. This morning I was beginning to lose hope. I felt trapped, on the edge. Now I can see that I have achieved a lot in my career. If I've done it before I can do it again. I just need to work out what the root causes of the problems and the possible options are," Joe admits, smiling at the contrast between how he felt ten minutes earlier and how he feels now.

Richard smiles too. Leaning towards Joe he lowers his voice and asks, "What makes a business successful: focusing on fixing problems and weaknesses or focusing on company strengths and opportunities?"

Joe considers the question for 30 seconds. "Probably both," he replies.

"Exactly!" continues Richard, "and what percentage of your time and that of your team is focused on the company's problems, as opposed to its core strengths and opportunities?"

"We definitely spend the majority of our time talking about problems," Joe admits without hesitation.

"So, let's imagine you switch this focus to spend 80% of your time and effort on your core strengths as a leader and the core strengths and opportunities of your team and this organisation. The remaining 20% of your time can be focused on reducing weaker areas and other performance risks," Richard picks up, displaying another slide on his screen.

Positive Balance

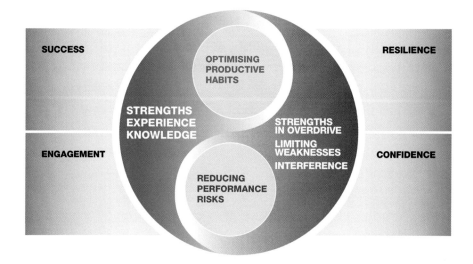

"You see it is all about ensuring the right balance. Research shows that if you spend 80% of your time and energy in this top half, optimising your productive habits, and 20% down here, reducing performance risks, you will grow in terms of successes, resilience, confidence and engagement," Richard explains.

"But we can't do that. We have too many problems at the

moment!" protests Joe, rubbing the back of his neck and looking down at the notes he has been making. "And what do you mean by performance risks? I remember you using this term on the plane as well?" he adds.

"Performance risks are things that limit or get in the way of progress. There are three main types:

1. Limiting weaknesses – things that you're not good at and don't enjoy but which, if not done, may stop progress.

2. Strengths in overdrive – things that you do enjoy and that you are good at but which, if used in the wrong way, at the wrong time or in the wrong amount, stop or limit progress.

3. Other sources of internal interference (those self-limiting beliefs or assumptions that have developed over time) or external sources (such as the culture of an organisation or the leadership style of its executives).

"Anyway, back to my original question Joe: what if you were to spend 80% of your time and effort focusing on strengths and 20% focussing on reducing weaker areas and performance risks?" Richard asks.

He remains silent waiting for Joe to look up again. As Joe does, Richard meets his eyes and holds his gaze. Joe realises that Richard is inviting him to reconsider what he has just said.

"Well, perhaps we can do both... I am starting to see that giving more attention to our strengths and opportunities might be really beneficial to get us off this precipice," contemplates Joe, rubbing the back of his neck again.

"Indeed," affirms Richard. "To get a team performing at the top of their game, it is crucial to focus on individual and collective strengths. Understanding and clearly communicating your own and your business's values, aspirations and abilities is vital too. The point where these four things meet is where you will find your Leadership Edge. The point at which the business's strengths, values, aspirations and abilities meet, is where you'll find the key to this business's expansion too. We will explore this in detail at our next session."

"Woah! Slow down," interrupts Joe, leaning back in his chair, both hands behind his head. He is clearly irritated. "So. You're now saying that strengths are just part of the picture. I can see from our discussion just now how focusing on strengths and successes, rather than weaknesses and failures might work, though I am still concerned that we do not just ignore our weaknesses. Also what about our failures? I know I've learned so much from mine. Surely reviewing failure – and lessons learned – is important, and you seem to be navigating totally away from this. In fact, this is beginning to sound increasingly unrealistic. And like it's going to take forever," vents Joe, rolling up his sleeves.

"My strengths, their strengths, values, aspirations, abilities and habits. Hell Richard, I've not got time for all this. And what about experience? Isn't the experience they bring to the business just as important as this stuff? I've a business to run here you know Richard. I haven't even got time to work out where to start!" Joe rants as he gets up from his chair and walks over to the window.

"Yes Joe. I know. This will help you run your business. Just think about it for a minute. What will happen if you continue down the path you are currently on? You described to me earlier a culture of mistrust and pessimism. I can see that the culture here tends to focus on short-term wins rather than long-term successes. It is clear that your energy level, and their energy levels," Richard gestures towards the glass partition to the open plan office, "are not high. You've described to me all their – and your – shortcomings. You also said that talking about your successes and your strengths felt 'energising'. That it made you feel less trapped, like there were more choices, yes?" he asks.

"Yes," replies Joe.

"Sure, people can learn a lot from failure and mistakes, but this is only half of the picture Joe – they also learn a lot from expanding their Comfort Zone. This is something that every leader needs to master to avoid the Path of Limitation™.

"So, your first choice Joe, is whether you want to get back onto that Path of Possibility™ we were talking about – or whether you want to return to the Path of Limitation™?"

"Before you answer, think about where your resistance is coming from. Is it just that you have got used to thinking in terms of failures and weaknesses, of fixing what's broken, rather than sharpening what's already great? Is it because you've been going down this path for so long that you've run out of steam and are unable to create choices? Where is this path going to lead you? And them?" Richard concludes, pointing towards Joe's colleagues.

"As to where to start, I'm mailing you a link to a leading online strengths profiling tool, called Strengthscope360™. I'm sending you a user name and a password too so you can access the tool. If you take around 20 minutes to do this, we can prepare an in-depth Strengths Profile, which will help you understand your productive strengths as well as providing you with feedback from your colleagues about how your strengths are viewed by them. The profile will help you to better understand your leadership style. It will suggest ways to sharpen your contribution to this business by, for example, stretching your strengths, harnessing productive energy, activating under-used strengths and practising the Stretch Leadership™ Habits.

"And by the way, stretching your strengths and using them more effectively, lending strengths to and borrowing strengths from your wider team, is exactly how successful organisations deal with what you call weaknesses," Richard adds.

"At our next session we'll review your profile, see what it tells us about where to find your Leadership Edge and look at the first Stretch Leadership™ Habit, *Sharing Vision*. We'll also look at how to reduce any performance risks that may result from failing to manage any of those weaknesses you are concerned about. OK?"

"Yes," replies Joe half-heartedly, his mind already reflecting on the question Richard has just posed about where he'll end up if he stays on his current path. He knows he doesn't want to but he is not yet convinced that he, or his organisation, is ready to be stretched in this way.

"That's OK but I'm not happy signing up to a six month contract yet. I want to see if this stuff works before committing. Can we come to a compromise Richard?" he continues after a pause.

"What sort of a compromise Joe?" asks an amused Richard.

"Well, can we trial this approach? Can I commit to, say three meetings, and we review if it's working before committing to the six months?"

"Sure Joe. We'll focus on identifying goals and getting some quick wins over the next six weeks. You'll soon see why this approach works," Richard reassures Joe. "One of the first positive patterns of behaviour to start mindfully practising is to fill in a Learning Journal at the end of each session. Here's a journal. Just jot down the key things you learned today and find some time during the week to reflect on what you write," Richard concludes as he hands over a Stretch Learning Journal to Joe, in which Joe is pleased to see copies of the models Richard introduced him to during the session.

"Yes Sir!" jokes Joe.

"Great!" smiles Richard, closing up his laptop and getting ready to leave.

Having said goodbye to Richard, Joe returns to his office. He has a call scheduled with his solicitor to talk about divorce proceedings.

'Remembering my successes did feel good. I wish Lynette would remember what I did right as well as what I did wrong,' he reflects as he accepts the call.

Joe's Learning Journal Entry

1. There's a different way to think about leading than the 'fix it' attitude I've become accustomed to. Focusing too firmly on given boundaries, weaknesses and failure may limit growth. Practising a strengths-based approach to leadership is, perhaps, a more positive way to engage stakeholders and get lasting success. I need to challenge my beliefs and weed out the unhealthy, self-limiting ones associated with the Path of Limitation™. I need to replace them with more positive, solutions-focused beliefs.

2. First I need to understand more about what I'm good at and what energises me (my strengths), and align these with my values, aspirations and abilities to find my Leadership Edge.

3. Then I need to make some behavioural changes to help me adopt the four Stretch Leadership™ Habits: Sharing Vision; Sparking Engagement; Skilfully Executing and Sustaining Progress. This will lead to a clearer sense of purpose, increased passion and engagement, more effective processes and improved performance and results.

4. Staying on the Path of Possibility™ will, hopefully, help me and the organisation to succeed, but only time will tell...

Chapter 2

Habit 1
Sharing Vision

In which Joe practises setting Stretch Goals...

"If you want to build a ship, don't drum up the men to gather wood, divide the work and give orders. Instead, teach them to yearn for the vast and endless sea."
Antoine de Saint-Exupery

Two weeks later, one late evening, Joe sits in his apartment assessing what he has learned from his first coaching session and the Strengthscope360™ Profile, which he has just received.

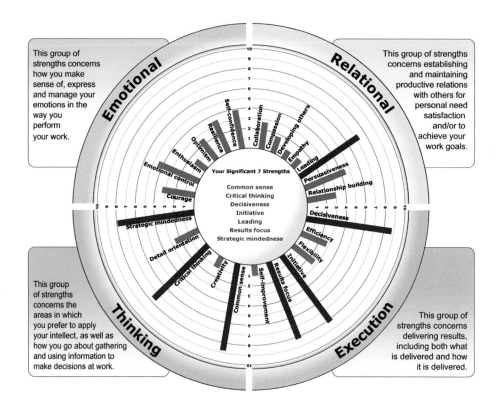

According to his Strengthscope360™ feedback report, his top strengths, described as his 'Significant Seven', are:

- *Critical Thinking*
- *Decisiveness*
- *Initiative*
- *Leading*
- *Results Focus*
- *Common Sense*
- *Strategic Mindedness*

Of these seven, several seem a bit vague, he will ask Richard about these at their next session, he decides. *Critical Thinking*, *Decisiveness*, *Leading* and *Results Focus* however, speak to him loud and clear.

'*Initiative*?' he ponders. 'Isn't initiative about ideas? I really wouldn't describe myself as an ideas person, but perhaps I'm going to need to be if I am to lead this team beyond the boundaries within which we're currently operating.'

Reading further into his report, Joe learns a new definition of initiative: 'taking independent action to make things happen and achieve goals'.

'OK,' he thinks, 'yes that fits.' Reading on though, he notes an observation from a colleague (the online assessment had asked him to nominate up to eight colleagues to provide feedback on his strengths). Apparently, he sometimes takes the initiative too quickly, without seeking the opinions or approval of those his actions might affect.

He is pleased to see the *Results Focus* strength, which he

recognises immediately. Seeing the description of the 'strength in overdrive' though, (which the report defines as 'a strength that can be overused to negative effect') is not so pleasing.

'Definition of Results Focus Strength in Overdrive: in your drive for results, you may miss important aspects of task/project success, e.g. the opportunity to reflect and learn, ensuring that people are engaged, and people are recognised for their efforts,' he reads.

Strategic Mindedness is another strength Joe is relieved to see in his profile. Reading that his colleagues are not currently seeing this strength being used productively though, comes as a bit of a shock.

In fact, focusing in further he sees some patterns developing, 'short-term focus' and 'lack of direction' being the key themes.

Joe stops reading the profile. He feels likes he's been hit in the chest by an oncoming vehicle that he did not see coming.

'I got the job for the exact strengths this profile highlights, so why aren't people seeing these strengths,' he ponders, trying to stop his thoughts racing.

He can't though. Reflecting on why his colleagues are not recognising what he perceives as his strengths triggers more of Joe's own thoughts about the day's events:

'What will the implications be if I do actually think less about the problems we are facing and more about the strengths and opportunities?'

'How will this impact team morale, my relationship with Kelly and corporate HQ and company performance?'

'Can any of these strengths help me out of my situation with Lynette?'

'Aren't the team going to think I'm a soft touch if I start babbling on about strengths, rather than targeting and removing our weaknesses, which are plain for everyone to see?'

'And, some of the team need a stick, not a carrot, to get them moving.'

'And what if we find people aren't playing to their strengths and that their strengths don't fit? Who's going to do the actual real stuff that needs doing if we are going to make up the gap and hit our target?'

These questions, and more, cascade into Joe's consciousness late into the night, until his *Results Focus* strength kicks in and he begins to formulate a plan in his mind for the coming week.

'Successful people focus on making their strengths productive and don't dwell on their weaknesses,' Richard had said. 'They take the Path of Possibility™, not the Path of Limitation™.' This is a revolutionary idea to Joe. He has been groomed to believe that improvement is all about fixing bad points and weaknesses. This is certainly what he had been taught at school, at home and throughout his career. He even uses this approach in raising his own kids, focusing on their lower grades when their report cards arrive at the end of term, rather than the 'A' grades, or at least encouraging a balance by looking at both. He is using it in his strategy for dealing with his broken marriage too.

Joe's thoughts spiral around his marriage and the children for a while, until he pulls back control, forcing himself to stop dwelling on his personal life and start addressing his professional one. Smiling to himself, Joe wonders what Kelly will make of all this strengths stuff. 'Not much,' he concludes.

Kelly is one of the toughest bosses Joe has ever worked for. She expects nothing short of excellence and keeps pushing for more, even in the face of a global economic downturn. 'She's just not going to get it,' he thinks, without recognising that the very thing he is annoyed with her about – her relentless pursuit for excellence – is one of his top values, an integral part of who he is, driving how he behaves. In fact, his own relentless drive for excellence pretty much got him into the situation from which he is currently trying to escape.

Joe suddenly feels overwhelmed by tiredness. Reflecting in this way does not come naturally to him. Switching off his computer, he goes to bed, hoping that he is tired enough to actually get a good night's sleep for a change.

*

The next morning, Joe is up and in the office even earlier than usual.

His first meeting is with Raj, who, no doubt, will complain about Mark's behaviour yesterday. Joe reflects on how to handle Raj and decides to take a new approach, inspired by what he had heard at yesterday's session. He chooses to suspend disbelief for the day.

As expected, Raj launches a barrage of complaints about Mark within the first few minutes of the meeting. Joe struggles to control his patience, but he listens carefully. When Raj finally finishes, he asks, "You and Mark have been working together for over two years now. Tell me about some of the successes you have shared?"

Raj, clearly exasperated, states abruptly, "That's not the point. I think he needs to be pulled into line or I'll have to consider my future with Tiger."

Joe realises this is going to be even harder than he had thought. "Just give this a try," he urges. "I want to understand your relationship better and how the current challenges have arisen."

"Ok, but I really don't see how this is going to help," Raj says, reluctantly. "Mark and I worked well together when I first started. We managed to launch the first website into the market in a record time of three months. We also launched the new agency module six months ago, which was a great success."

Encouraged by the noticeable softening in Raj's attitude, Joe pushes further. "What strengths did you guys use to achieve those results? By strengths I mean personal qualities that made you feel energised and led to you doing great work," clarifies Joe remembering the very specific definition of strengths he had read in his profile the night before.

"That's a tough question," responds Raj. "I suppose I am good at organising and planning. I enjoy working out how to do things (and how not to do them) and I find it easy. Mark is not good at this. He just doesn't do details. He's really good with people though. It's clear he enjoys talking with our customers, and he's good at it. He gets all sorts of information from them that I would never be able to. He's a very creative thinker, whereas I'm more of a logical thinker, I guess."

Raj falls silent for a while, reflecting on what he has just said. "Come to think of it, we do have strengths and skills that complement each other, but we can't seem to communicate with each other anymore, even at a basic level. These days, working with him just exhausts me."

Joe realises he will have to dig deep to help Raj and Mark find a way forward. If he doesn't he'll be risking losing one (or both) of them from the business. With Robert's departure, he simply could not afford to allow this to happen.

"OK," Joe says, standing up and walking to join Raj on the other side of the desk. "I have an idea that might get your relationship back on track. Do you want to hear about it?"

"Why not?" asks Raj, not sounding terribly committed, though secretly intrigued by what his boss is about to say. "We've tried everything else recently. Even Gwen in HR had a go at helping us, so you may as well throw your ideas into the ring," he adds.

Joe decides to go for it.

"I'd like you and Mark to think about your successes over the past two years and the strengths and skills you used when your relationship was, shall we say, more 'productive'. I'd also like you to think about how you can use these strengths, and your past achievements, perhaps borrowing from each other's strengths to get your relationship back on track. I suggest you both take a couple of days to do this and each write down key points and insights to bring along to a meeting with me. We can then discuss how you get past your current difficulties and move forward, using the web site rebrand as a project. I will try to get Mark's commitment to do this too and I will let you know the minute I know his thoughts."

Raj looks at Joe, bemused, and says, "Ok, I'm willing to give it a try, but I warn you, I'm not holding out much hope."

Joe thanks Raj and, after Raj has left the office, returns to his chair wondering if he has done the right thing.

'I know exactly what's the matter with those two. They just wind each other up and always will. One of them needs to go. Why am I playing around with this strengths stuff? If I get them to do it, I'll have to get the others to do it as well. It will be anarchy with everyone running around trying to identify their strengths and nobody focussing on hitting our targets.

'Still, *if you always do what you've always done, you always get what you always got,* as Lynette says. At least this is a different approach,' he thinks. 'What's the worst that can happen? '

Little does Joe know that he has just, in Richard's language, 'stretched' his *Decisiveness, Initiative* and *Critical Thinking* strengths, combining them in a new way and pushing himself beyond his 'Comfort Zone'. He has also tasked Raj and Mark with a Stretch Project...

*

"So Joe, how was your week?" asks Richard as he enters Joe's office.

"Well, I could quote Vinny Jones' character in *Lock, Stock and Two Smoking Barrels*, 'It's been emotional,' but as you will see from my Strengthscope360™ report, I'm not exactly an emotional person. So, let's just say 'It's been thought provoking' shall we?" states Joe in a tone that implies humour yet clearly masks anxiety.

"Ah, so you spotted that most of your standout strengths lie in the bottom two clusters of the 'strengths wheel', meaning that you are more task focused than people focused?" asks Richard.

"Yes. And of course I am more task focused than people focused at work. I'm meant to be a leader and leaders focus on tasks and results. I employ other people, like Gwen, to do the people stuff," Joe replies, rather confrontationally.

"I'm more people focused in my personal life though," he continues, his tone softening as he suddenly realises that his personal life is fast becoming non-existent.

"So there are two yous are there Joe? The professional you and the at home you?" Richard prompts.

"I suppose so," replies Joe.

"Or is it that there is only one you, you have just learned to express yourself differently in different situations because of what you think is valued in each context?"

Joe just looks at Richard. He makes no response. Richard, aware that Joe is processing a lot of information and supressed emotion, continues on.

"Great teams are made up of people with strengths from each cluster in this wheel." Richard pulls up a slide.

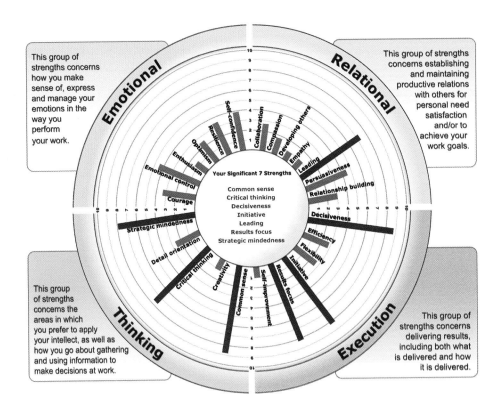

"Nobody can be strong in all these areas. There is no such thing as a well-rounded leader. Every leader has areas of strength and areas of limitation. Great leaders recognise what they do and don't have and call on the strengths of those around them to make up for their limitations. Being strong isn't about being self-sufficient. Strong people and strong teams know how to borrow strengths from, and lend strengths to, other people. In the natural world this is called interdependence. There is a lot we can learn from the natural world. Setting up successful businesses is not dissimilar to setting up successful ecosystems. At the end of the day, everything needs homeostasis – or balance – to thrive.

"Think of a soccer team. You wouldn't play Lionel Messi or David Beckham in goal would you? Soccer teams collectively cover each position on the pitch. The best teams have each player in a position that plays to their strengths. The best business teams collectively cover each area of the strengths wheel, with each team member in a role that plays to their strengths. Get this right and you've everything you need to move beyond any boundary or obstacle, real or perceived. You will be able to move in whichever direction you set," adds Richard, neatly bringing the conversation round to the subject of setting Stretch Goals – an important behavioural pattern associated with the first Stretch Leadership™ Habit, *Sharing Vision*, and the planned topic for the session.

"And to ensure you achieve even the most challenging goals," he adds purposefully, watching Joe practising his subconscious habit of rolling up his sleeves. 'It's as if he's preparing for an operation,' thinks Richard.

Joe absorbs the words on the slide. He is already feeling

comforted, recognising that members of his leadership team do indeed have some of the strengths from the top of the slide, the strengths he, apparently, lacks.

"So, I said last week that we'd review your Strengths Profile before trying to find your Leadership Edge and learning about the first Stretch Leadership™ Habit – *Sharing Vision*. Let's take a look at it. Did you recognise yourself? Have you noticed yourself using any of these strengths this week?"

Joe goes on to describe his thoughts about the strengths he recognises and the ones he doesn't. Typically, Joe starts by focusing on what he does not recognise, what he does not like or agree with. Richard skilfully guides him towards recognising and celebrating the strengths that he has and the power he has to dial them up and down, according to the needs of specific situations.

"It's kind of like turning the volume up and down on a radio. You can have it on as loud as you like when you're alone and not trying to focus on anything else. When you're in a public place, such as on a train or in a park though, it's always wise to exercise caution and understanding of the needs of others."

Feeling encouraged, Joe tells Richard about his new approach with Raj and Mark. Richard immediately picks up on this.

"Ah, well there you go, you say you do not see *Initiative* as a strength, yet did you not use your *Initiative* in finding a new way to look at the issues caused by Raj and Mark's working relationship?"

"Well, I guess that's one way of looking at it," Joe says thoughtfully.

"In fact you did more than exercise your *Initiative* strength. You combined it with two of your standout strengths, the strengths that really describe who you are, *Decisiveness* and *Critical Thinking*, in a totally new way. That is what we call 'Stretch'. You stretch your strengths by using them in a new way, outside of your Comfort Zone. It's one way to overcome obstacles or barriers, Joe, and you're already doing it intuitively. Not only are you stretching yourself Joe, you have also set two members of your leadership team a Stretch Project. This is good!" Richard enthuses.

Joe smiles. Things had actually been going quite well with the Raj/Mark situation and Joe was already seeing the benefits of his new approach.

"We'll talk more about this later and about how to optimise your strengths, and those of your colleagues, as well as how to deal with any performance risks these strengths in overdrive (or any lack of strengths) may cause. First though, let's investigate your 'Leadership Brand': who you are; what you bring to this organisation; what difference you want to make here and how you want people to view you as a leader," says Richard, pulling up a slide on his screen that looked similar to the type of brand pyramid Joe was more familiar with as a marketing communications tool.

Leadership Brand

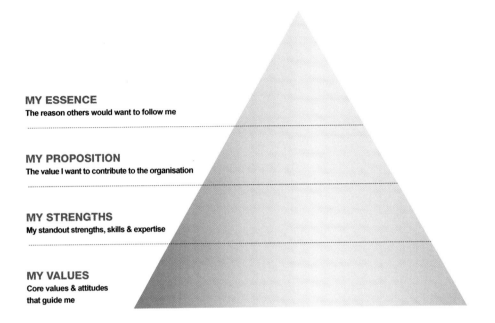

MY ESSENCE
The reason others would want to follow me

MY PROPOSITION
The value I want to contribute to the organisation

MY STRENGTHS
My standout strengths, skills & expertise

MY VALUES
Core values & attitudes
that guide me

Joe and Richard begin working through the slide together, starting at the bottom and working up.

"I'm not sure how to describe my values, I know that I always want people to be up front and honest with me, I can't stand it when people don't tell you the truth and you don't know what you are dealing with," contemplates Joe.

"So, do you think one of your values is 'truth'?" suggests Richard.

"Don't know. That doesn't quite fit. I just want people to own up and be honest if a mistake is made," Joe responds.

"Perhaps it's 'honesty' then?" clarifies Richard.

"Yes, that seems more like what I'm describing," agrees Joe.

"OK, so what else, what is really important to you about the way you work with people and how they work with you?" pushes Richard.

"Well, I can't stand people who aren't focused, who seem to dawdle when there is no need. I like people to care and have a sense of urgency - we need to react and act quickly. There are times to be thoughtful but on the whole I can't stand it when people just don't get on with things," Joe explains.

"So is it about being 'focused', that was a word you just used?"

"It's more than that, it's about going at speed, picking up the pace," Joe is living his value without realising it. Before Richard has a chance to make another suggestion, Joe exclaims: "That's it, 'pace'. I want us all to have pace, not feel rushed but just to work at pace. But I also value people with integrity, hard-workers, team workers. I value determination, commitment, I could think of lots more words, it's really hard to identify just a few!"

"Yes I understand that. How about we decide on a few now and you take the list away and do a bit more thinking on it. The best way to get clarity is to rank your values in order of importance. Remember that values are your internal compass: they guide the way you behave. So if you're struggling to order them, think about a real and difficult situation you are in and ask yourself, 'which of these values can help me navigate my way through?' Try to distil down to three or four values, like four points on a compass," Richard summarises.

Working through his Significant Seven strengths, as identified in his Strengths Profile, Joe identifies his Standout Strengths as *Critical Thinking*, *Decisiveness* and *Results Focus*. He adds 'market knowledge' and 'broad business experience' as the specific skills and expertise he brings to the organisation.

Moving up to the next level though, Joe begins to struggle.

"I'm not sure I understand the difference between my legacy and my essence, aren't they saying the same thing?" Joe asks.

"You're right, they are, but what's different is who they are targeted at. The legacy is mainly for you. It is your way of describing the difference you wish to make; the value you intend to bring. The essence is for other people. It reflects how you want your leadership value to be described by others in 10 to 15 seconds." Richard clarifies.

"Oh right. How should I go about deciding on what my legacy is, there are so many things I'd like to achieve?" Joe responds.

"Well, it's the one thing you want to be remembered for. What do you care most about? If there was one thing people remembered you for, what would it be?" guides Richard.

"Wow that's a hard one. That's like blowing my own trumpet, and I'm not sure I'm comfortable with that. Who am I to say that I will be memorable and what happens if people don't remember me for what I want to be remembered for?" Joe stalls.

"That's a very normal and natural reaction to the question Joe. Try looking at it another way: if you don't know where you are going, how will you know when you have got there? If you don't define a goal, how will you know what to focus your energy on? One of your strengths is *Results Focus* isn't it? This is all about applying that strength to defining and achieving your personal brand. How do you apply your *Results Focus* strength to work tasks?" Richard pushes.

Joe looks thoughtful and does not speak for at least a minute. The silence is palpable but comfortable.

"I guess you're right. At work I clearly define what we want to achieve with the team and then I go all out to damn well make sure we achieve it," is his eventual response.

"So could you apply that here? How do you decide what to focus on at work? There must be lots of things that need to be done, how do you decide which goals to set?" Richard prompts.

"Well, the most important and pressing," replies Joe as if he thinks the answer is obvious.

"So what's the most important and pressing thing that you want to do as a leader?" persists Richard.

"Well, it's about people I think. It's about getting people to work together and achieve more than they could have imagined," Joe summarises.

"So, how do you want to be remembered Joe?" asks Richard, smiling inwardly as he remembers Joe's earlier comment about employing other people to do 'the people stuff'.

"As a deliverer who made teams work to produce exceptional results," concludes Joe.

"And how can you express this as a motto, a motivational call to action that will engage your team to do their best for you? What is your essence?"

"Something like: *delivering the best, together,*" Joe responds.

Reviewing the completed pyramid on his screen, Richard is curious about the legacy Joe wishes to leave at Tiger. With

Joe's Leadership Brand

MY ESSENCE The reason others would want to follow me	Delivering the best, together
MY PROPOSITION The value I want to contribute to the organisation	To deliver quality products through motivating teams to produce exceptional results
MY STRENGTHS My standout strengths, skills & expertise	Critical Thinking Decisiveness Results Focus Broad Business Market knowledge Experience
MY VALUES Core values & attitudes that guide me	Excellence Pace Honesty Positive Contribution

further prompting about what a good team looks like, Joe describes a thriving business where people show up at work wanting to do their very best, enjoy what they do and always meet their targets.

"So you want to create a thriving business where people bring the best of themselves to work, enjoy what they do and always hit their targets, yes?" asks Richard.

"Yup," nods Joe.

"So, for someone who is task focused, I am interested in why you think it is important for people to enjoy their work?" Richard probes, delighted at the speed with which Joe seems to be navigating towards the Path of Possibility™.

"Because if people enjoy what they do, it is not a struggle. They feel upbeat and energised and this positive energy becomes 'the norm', the way things are done. With an environment where there is positive energy, things get done. Targets get met. It's as simple as that," responds Joe, surprised at how enthusiastic he is feeling.

"I guess it's what you call taking the Path of Possibility™," he adds thoughtfully. "I want to lead people towards this path. I've had enough of uphill battles and getting stuck in a swamp of problems and poor morale. It's about time we stopped being victims here and show ourselves to be capable of growth."

"Good. You are already thinking like the leader of a top team. You have a good understanding of who you are as a leader and hopefully this pyramid will help you to communicate that to your team. Once they know what you expect of them – and what they should expect from you – your role as a leader will become easier. It will become easier still if you take a close look at your team's Strengthscope360™ Profiles to ensure that you have everything you need to realise your vision.

"Then all you need to do is to share your vision by creating a 'Picture of Success', a rallying call that will inspire and motivate your team to want to join the journey. We'll talk about this later, how to express a vision, or a mission, in a way that will take people along with you. First though, you need to focus on the end result, where it is you want to take your team. So, let's have a look at how to set Stretch Goals.

"What do you think a Stretch Goal is Joe?" Richard asks.

"A goal that challenges you to push yourself beyond where you are," suggests Joe, thinking as he says this that all goals are designed to do that, making the word 'stretch' kind of redundant.

"Yes. It is more than that though. It is a goal that positively challenges you to move beyond your Comfort Zone by stretching your strengths and expertise to achieve new, clearly identified heights. Successful organisations set 'Individual Stretch Goals' for each member of staff as part of their personal development programme, 'Team Stretch Goals' and 'Organisational Stretch Goals'. This enables them to move beyond the 'Point of Stretch' to the 'Zone of Stretch and Peak Performance'.

Richard reveals another slide.

The Stretch Zone

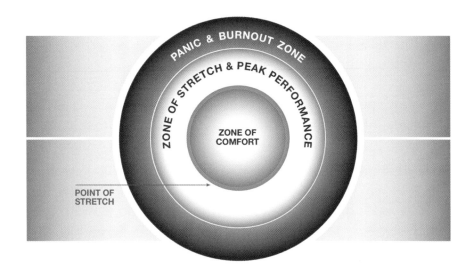

Picking up an elastic band, Richard holds up his left hand, the band loosely draped over his thumb and index finger. Moving his finger and thumb apart, he stretches the band so that the edges are straight but not tight.

"Stretch Goals take you from here, your Zone of Comfort, to here," he moves his fingers apart stretching the band further, "The Point of Stretch. To here," his fingers are as far apart as they can get – almost – the band stretching to its limits, "The Zone of Stretch and Peak Performance.

"The art of setting Stretch Goals is to take yourself, your team and your organisation to here, but not to," Richard stretches his finger and thumb that extra few millimetres apart and the band snaps "here – the Burnout and Panic Zone," he concludes.

"The way to do this is to practice the four Stretch Leadership™ Habits. OK?" checks Richard.

"OK," replies Joe, looking down at the broken band. He has never empathised with an item of stationery before.

"Good. Now, you are already setting Stretch Goals for your team – that project you gave to Raj and Mark is a Stretch Project. What do you think the Stretch Goal for it might have been if you had formally set it up as a Stretch Project?"

"To combine their strengths in a way that compensated for their weaknesses in order to deliver the rebrand of the web site on time and within budget?" suggests Joe.

"Good, but when communicating goals, or a corporate vision come to that, try starting at the end – the outcome you want. That's where all peak performers start in all walks of life – by clearly identifying their goal – the trophy they wish to lift. They then work backwards to where they are now, in order to work out how to get there. Try being specific about the details too, the timings and the costs here, for example," Richard advises.

"So, 'to deliver a rebranded website by the end of the quarter for under £20,000, combining the team's individual strengths, skills and expertise' perhaps?" clarifies Joe, picking up on the language used in his Strengthscope360™ Profile, and by Richard.

"Excellent," encourages Richard. "The key is to set people Stretch Goals that challenge them to perform to the peak of their capability. This isn't about cracking the whip and working people harder to meet short-term results, which can actually be demotivating and demoralising. It's about setting an ambitious Picture of Success for the organisation that people can relate to and breaking work down into manageable phases, or Stretch Goals, that people find inspiring and morale boosting."

"Have you heard about the Eliza Doolittle Principle?" continues Richard.

Joe ponders the question for a while before answering "Is that from *My Fair Lady*, when the pompous British linguist turns a flower girl into a lady? I remember seeing the stage show in London's West End years ago."

"That's the one," replies Richard. "The underlying principle is the important thing I want to stress here: people will perform to the level of expectations which are created for them. This is an incredibly powerful effect that has been proven through several decades of research. So, if leaders have positive, stretching expectations of their staff, they will generally live up to these, and even over-deliver. This is illustrated in *My Fair Lady,* as Eliza Doolittle starts to become a lady when Professor Higgins' attitude and behaviour towards her shifts and reflects the belief that she can, despite all odds, become a lady reflecting elite London society. Conversely, if you have negative expectations of people, they are likely to perform *down* to these negative expectations."

"I think I get it. So, if we set challenging and realistic Stretch Goals for people and reinforce through our words and actions that we expect them to achieve these, they will generally meet or surpass those goals," reflects Joe.

"Absolutely," responds Richard, "one of the crucial roles of any leader is to set the expectation that everyone can, and should, become better and better."

"So how about a Stretch Project for you Joe? What might your Stretch Goal be, taking into account that legacy we've been talking about. Let's start there – at the end – how you want to be remembered," Richard pushes on.

Twenty minutes later and Joe feels invigorated. Working from the end to the beginning intrigues him. It reminds him of how he had worked out his training schedule when he'd run a marathon ten years earlier, before he'd had children. It reminds him of a speech he'd once heard the Olympic rower, Sir Steve Redgrave, give about winning rituals and routines. It gives him an idea about how to create some happy memories for his children too – a family Stretch Project. Joe is in his element.

"How are you feeling Joe?" asks Richard, as Joe purposefully adds a full stop to the final Leadership Stretch Goal he has just identified for himself:

Long-term Stretch Goal: Within the next three years, to create a business with key talent retention rates of 90%, employee satisfaction rates of 85%, where revenue has increased by 150% and profit has increased by 40%, through aligning individuals' strengths to their roles and creating a culture where individuals combine their strengths to get the job done.

Medium-term Stretch Goal: By the end of the year, to align the job roles of my leadership team to their strengths, according to the outcomes of their Stretch Projects, in a way that will continue the drive towards a 50% revenue growth target by year end.

Short-term Stretch Goal: By the end of the quarter, to profile the strengths of my leadership team and set each of them a Stretch Goal that will drive towards a 25% revenue growth target by end quarter.

"Buzzing!" Joe replies, "Like I need to start clarifying all this and communicating it with the rest of the leadership team, drawing on their strengths to help me, of course."

"Great! And communicating 'all this' is about more than writing the sort of mission and vision statement you can pull a template off the internet for. It's about collectively nailing a Picture of Success, describing what it's actually going to look and feel like when you – collectively – reach your goals. But, again, we are jumping ahead!" Richard concludes, delighted that Joe seems to be getting it so quickly.

"So Joe, you may not realise it yet, but you're finding your way along this pathway intuitively. You've already picked up yourself that your *Decisiveness* strength may lead to you making decisions based on short-term outcomes, for example. This is something we'll work on next week, when we'll learn about the second behavioural pattern that will embed the *Sharing Vision* habit: optimising strengths."

Returning to his office after saying goodbye to Richard, Joe is struck by Richard's earlier comment about being strong is not the same as being self-sufficient. It echoes one of Lynette's mantras:

"Marriage is meant to be a partnership, Joe. I'm fed up of making these decisions alone then being criticised for getting it wrong. If you want to be in control, try turning up sometimes. Either that or go! It would actually be easier being a single parent."

Joe picks up the phone to Lynette. He thinks it is probably a good idea to get her feedback and buy-in to the project he has in mind for the kids, and now he has it in mind, he doesn't want to hang about...

Joe's Learning Journal Entry

1. I've clarified my Leadership Essence and reclaimed my Leadership Edge. It feels like our organisational values are similar to my personal values, so I do belong here. My personal values are certainly aligned with Kelly's values. Maybe I find her so frustrating because she reminds me that I am not living my values?

2. I do actually believe that I can use my personal strengths, and our collective strengths, to get us out of the mess we are in. I am going to need to chunk it up though into short, medium and long-term Stretch Goals, and not allow the big picture to be jeopardised by short-term thinking. People think that I act too quickly without bringing in others early enough sometimes. This may be because my Decisiveness strength can lead me away from the long-term goal and cause me to act independently.

3. My Standout Strengths are: Results Focus, Critical Thinking and Decisiveness. I may need to dial some of these down sometimes, such as my Decisiveness strength. I may also need to combine these with some of my colleagues' Standout Strengths sometimes to overcome some of my weaknesses. They can borrow from my strengths store too, to overcome theirs. We just need to understand more about each other's strengths and these dynamics to do this.

4. I need to build support for a shared future by

clarifying and communicating all of this in a way that describes what it's going to look and feel like when we reach our goals.

5. All of the above relates to setting Stretch Goals – an important part of Sharing Vision. This is the first Stretch Leadership™ Habit. If I deliberately and diligently practice setting Stretch Goals, Sharing Vision will soon become second nature.

Chapter 3

Habit 1:
Sharing Vision, continued...

In which Joe practises optimising his strengths...

"We are always more anxious to be distinguished for a talent which we do not possess, than to be praised for the fifteen which we do possess."
Mark Twain, *Mark Twain's Autobiography*

Joe's meeting with Richard is to start 15 minutes late. He is stuck on a call with Kelly, who is giving him an earful about the previous month's sales, which are 8% down on the month before. Kelly is clearly not satisfied with his explanation and has little sympathy for the staff problems he is experiencing. She is about to drop a bombshell…

"We gave you this job because we felt you had the leadership ability to deal with these issues Joe, so don't bring me complaints about your team. You know you have the authority to hire and fire team members, so, if they're not working out, get in people who have the right skills and attitude to get the job done. There is only one proviso, and this is something you are going to have to share with the rest of your staff, just as all the other regional heads are, because they're all missing their targets: we're having to cut budgets, so you cannot make any pay increases, or pay any commission related bonuses, even if a member of your team meets their individual target. We're all in this together Joe. Got it?" asserts Kelly.

"Got it," replies Joe, after a short pause, uncharacteristically struggling to find words.

*

Kelly's harsh words still ringing in his ear, Joe sits down for his two-hour session with Richard.

"You don't look terribly happy Joe," observes Richard.

"No. My head is spinning. I've just had another balling-out from my boss, Kelly. She doesn't appreciate the problems I have here in Europe. This is a different market than the US. She just doesn't get the cultural differences. She expects me to tell my team that there is a pay freeze and no commission will be paid, even if they meet their targets! This is a commission-based business. How on earth she expects me to motivate them without the money incentive I really do not know," Joe vents.

Richard had planned to start by reviewing Joe's progress against the Stretch Goals he had set himself in the previous session. However, given the mood Joe is in and the conversation he has just had with Kelly, Richard decides to change tack and help Joe understand how he can optimise his strengths to move himself back towards the Path of Possibility™.

"OK Joe, the good news is that there are plenty of ways to motivate people, other than with money. Research shows that motivation stemming from within, what psychologists refer to as intrinsic motivation, is more sustainable too. The key is getting your team to share and believe in a vision and ensure that they are provided with opportunities to apply and stretch their strengths in a way that contributes to this vision. This is a vital part of the first Stretch Leadership™ Habit, which is what today's session is going to focus on. OK?"

"OK," sighs a subdued Joe.

"Optimising strengths – those of your team as well as your

own – is a key behaviour you need to build into your routine if you are going to embed all the leadership habits, but especially the first habit, *Sharing Vision*. Effective leadership is about stretching yourself, your team and the organisation. Optimising strengths is the starting point.

"Now is the perfect time to start optimising strengths Joe. You're already practising this subconsciously to some extent, by the end of this session you'll understand exactly what you can do to get these guys motivated, regardless of the bad news about the pay freeze. Ready?"

"Go on," prompts Joe, genuinely keen to hear what Richard will say next, yet but struggling to concentrate on the words coming out of Richard's mouth since the words he's just heard from Kelly are still echoing in his head.

"Remember the conversation we had in our first session about this coaching process taking you from aspirations to awareness, to action, to agility to achievement and then to revisit your aspirations? Let's try to use your current situation with Kelly to move from awareness to action. Ready?" asks Richard.

"OK," Joe mutters, slipping back into reluctant mode whilst rolling up his sleeves.

"So what do you value about Kelly as a boss Joe? What are her strengths?" invites Richard.

Joe's face drops. He is still livid about the conversation with Kelly and really wants a sympathetic ear, not an inquiring tongue. Still, he pulls himself round quickly enough, lifting his head and answering: "Well, Kelly's one of the smartest people I know. She totally understands the online recruitment business and gives me loads of rope to do what I want. She will not accept excuses or second bests, so I guess she shares some of my strengths – like *Leading*, *Results Focus* and *Strategic Mindedness*."

"Taking into account what you have just said about her strengths, and what you now know about your own strengths, what style is going to work best with her, what do you need to do to play to your collective strengths?" inquires Richard.

"I suppose I need to take more accountability. I need to take solutions to Kelly, rather than problems. I also need to ensure I know my stuff and am well prepared for our conversations. However, I always feel she's not the most approachable person; it's weird but I am unusually anxious when she's around. I would love to tap into her competitor and industry knowledge and insights, but feel I can't ask her for help with this."

Richard smiles, aware that Joe is already moving away from his pattern of self-reliance, in his mind at least. Since re-inventing himself as a strengths coach he has seen many successes. Even so, he still enjoys the rush of excitement he feels every time he senses these familiar turning points.

"Why is that Joe? Why do you feel you can't ask Kelly for help?" he prompts.

Joe looks at the floor, as if he keeps a store cupboard of answers there. After a long pause, he replies:

"I don't want her to know what I don't know. It makes me look weak."

"Ok, let's be practical about this. *Common Sense* is one of your strengths, let's use it to see if we can move ourselves across to the Path of Possibility™. Based on what you have told me about Kelly, you share some strengths, and certainly share some values, so can you try and empathise with her for a moment? If a direct report came to you and asked for advice or help, how would you feel?"

"I'd be pleased they'd shown initiative and I'd jump at the chance to share my knowledge. Being Results Focused and Strategically Minded, I love any opportunity to help fix things," responds Joe, bringing his gaze up to table level.

"And which strengths did you say you shared with Kelly?"

"*Leading, Results Focus* and *Strategic Mindedness,*" responds Joe, meeting Richard's eyes.

"So how do you think she'd respond to being asked for help?"

"She'd love it at the time. But after helping, she may judge me for not knowing my stuff in the first place," Joe responds, his *Critical Thinking* strength entering overdrive.

"Would you judge a member of your team in this situation?" asks Richard.

"Only if they hadn't thought it through properly in the first place, had come to me with something non-specific or meaningless which added no value to the outcomes we're driving towards."

"So, what are you going to do about approaching Kelly and tapping into her industry knowledge?" Richard pushes.

"I'm going to work out, exactly, what it is I want to learn from her and why, then go to her with specific, well thought out, questions."

"So how do you feel about Kelly now and asking her for help?" prompts Richard.

"Well, I can see how my assumptions about how she would react are just that, assumptions. In fact she may react how I would react. I think I just need to put a bit of thought into it before I approach her, which is fair enough," Joe replies.

"That all sounds good, and how do you feel?"

"More able to deal with it actually, not so afraid or anxious about it. Well, maybe still a bit afraid," says Joe with a wry smile, "but definitely more confident to do it."

"Good. Perhaps this is a good time to talk about how to ensure you are managing the potential consequences of any performance risks this team's individual and shared strengths may present. Can you remember what the three types of performance risk are? We talked about them at our last session." Richard pulls up Joe's Strengthscope360™ profile to help along their discussion.

"Yes 'limiting weaknesses', 'strengths in overdrive' and external and internal 'sources of interference'," Joe responds, not in the mood to go into detail as he wants to move forward, not reflect on last week's learning.

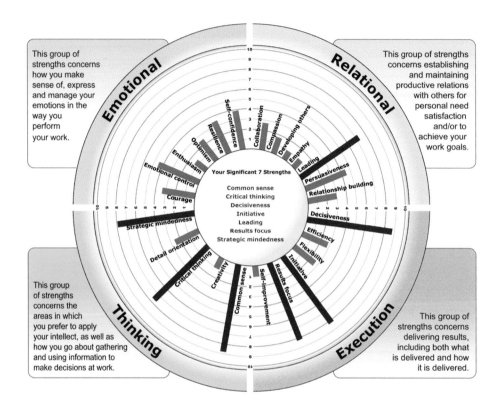

Realising that Joe may be able to repeat learning parrot fashion, but was not yet fully absorbing the learning and putting it into practice, Richard decides to persevere.

"To be effective, strengths need to be matched to the requirements of the situation. Leaders need to watch out for unintended consequences associated with strengths, which can easily arise. Let's look at the first performance risk, 'limiting weaknesses'. Do you think you have any limiting weaknesses Joe?" probes Richard.

"Well yes. I am not creative, developing others does not

come naturally to me – so not being able to offer pay related rewards kind of leaves me toothless, and, before you point it out to me, yes I know, optimism is not one of my strengths," Joe responds, a little defensively.

Richard realises that he is right. Joe is not yet understanding which weaknesses are limiting.

"OK. So some of these are not necessarily limiting weaknesses Joe. Some are allowable. Weaknesses are only limiting if they genuinely stop you from performing at your best. Weaknesses that do not impact your ability to do your job are allowable, so maybe you need to be a bit easier on yourself Joe. That said, how do you think you could manage the consequences of these weaknesses Joe?"

"Well I guess I need to work out which are allowable and look for ways to call on the strengths of those around me to compensate for those which aren't. I need to give this more thought, but *Developing Others* is probably a limiting weakness. The rest may be allowable," Joe responds in a tone that seems to lack his characteristic decisiveness.

"Good insight Joe. How about the next area of performance risk: strengths in overdrive? Let's work through an example. In our previous session, you mentioned your *Decisiveness* strength going into overdrive. Can you think of a time where you have used your *Decisiveness* strength and it hasn't yielded the result you expected?"

"I can think of a good example," Joe responds immediately, intrigued by this concept. "In our last management meeting, we were discussing what to do about a big client that has recently restructured into multiple divisions. We currently have one account manager responsible for all sales for this client, but Mark suggested we consider alternatives, for example, having different account managers for each line of business. I was quick to pass judgement in this case as I think Trevor, the current account manager, is doing an excellent job managing the account.

"However, now I wonder if this is the right decision, as the client has communicated that it will have different recruitment leads for each division and I'm not sure Trevor can service all these people effectively."

"So what will you do differently if a similar situation arises in future?" asks Richard.

"I will spend more time thinking about whether it is appropriate to use my *Decisiveness* strength," replies Joe, whose mind is already playing over similar scenarios in the recent past. "I'll consider whether I can dial up one of my other strengths, my *Common Sense* strength for example, instead. I'll listen more actively to what others are saying and consider calling on one of my more people-oriented colleague's strengths. If none of this leads us to where we need to be, I'll press the *Decisiveness* button," he concludes.

"So, to summarise, you will flex your style and your strengths to get the most out of each situation, orientating yourself, and your team along the Path of Possibility™. You will need to practice this behaviour if you are to stay on this path though Joe. The thing about habits is that bad ones are far easier to keep than good ones. The good news though, is that new habits are easy to create, and that all you need to do to embed new habits is to intentionally practice them regularly for several months.

"Great, now let's talk about the final area of performance risk: sources of interference. It will help here if you are actually aware of what your specific interferences are – internal and external – and how you can use your strengths to deal with them more effectively," Richard presses on.

Joe, trying to depersonalise the conversation, immediately starts to list the challenges the organisation faces. He explains that one of his challenges is that Tiger doesn't have a clear strategy for dealing with Dragon Jobs, its biggest rival in Europe. Dragon had a much more established brand, particularly in the UK, Europe's most lucrative online jobs market. He also cites relationship problems in the team and Robert's departure to Dragon as additional problem areas he needs to tackle.

"So, to clarify..." interjects Richard, moving across Joe's office to a flip chart, where he lifts up a pen and gets ready to write.

"You, as the leader of this organisation, are facing several challenges. These are:

1. *Sales are 25% behind target.*
2. *Several major accounts have not renewed contracts.*
3. *Relationships between colleagues are poor. There's a culture of mistrust and politicking.*
4. *The business's top performer has left to join your main competitor.*
5. *The business has no clear strategy for dealing with your main competitor.*

6. *You, currently, have no clear strategy for salvaging this year's performance and your boss has asked you to come up with one.*
7. *You are unable to use pay or performance related bonuses as an incentive to drive your team's performance.*

"Anything else?"

Joe leans back in his chair, hands behind his head, looking thoughtfully at the list on the flip chart. Seeing his challenges there, so clearly stated, is surprisingly comforting.

"No, that about sums it up," he replies.

"OK. Have you spoken to your leadership team about these challenges?"

"Well..." Joe speaks slowly, looking up as if he has left the answer to this question somewhere on the ceiling.

"Kind of, but maybe I have not communicated these problems with enough urgency, or in a way that encourages the team to come back with solutions. Maybe, if we did this as a group exercise, drawing on our collective strengths, we'd find a way forward," he continues.

"Good. So we are now ready to clarify a source of internal interference which appears to be frustrating your progress," points out Richard. "In order to achieve the Stretch Goals we discussed last week, you will need to stop believing you need to resolve all the challenges yourself and engage the whole team in finding solutions," continues Richard.

"We could, but is that going to help me work around the pay freeze dilemma Richard? I'm not sure you understand how big a deal a pay freeze is in a commissions based culture. I know the goals we set last week are important. I know that textbook management says to focus on the long-term. But I don't work in a textbook. I work in the real world and this short-term pay freeze thing is a real problem Richard. I need to deal with it," asserts Joe, his *Decisiveness* strength kicking in.

"OK. Let's look at the short term first then Joe. Remember what your short-term Stretch Goal is?" Richard responds, calmly.

"Profiling the strengths of my team and setting them Stretch Goals," Joe remembers.

"Do you think that focusing on this, enabling your team to tap into their natural energies and strengths might help them to understand that this is a short-term pain that can be overcome by excellent teamwork?" Richard asks.

"Some of them, perhaps," replies Joe, looking out towards his team, as if trying to work out which of them, if any, would really buy into this.

"Another good insight Joe. Different people will react to the news about the pay freeze in different ways, depending on their personality, strengths, values and how they are told about it. It's going to be important to listen to all of their views and opinions. Do you agree that understanding more about their strengths will help you to work out how to tell them, and, more importantly, will help you to bring the full power of their combined strengths to the table to find a solution to this situation?" Richard asks, slowing down his speech as he comes to the end of the sentence.

"Yes," Joe replies, almost before Richard has finished the sentence.

"So, let's get their Strengthscope360™ profiles, and once we understand more about them, why don't I make the focus of the next management meeting finding a solution to these pay freeze problems?" concludes Joe.

"Great idea – but maybe you can rephrase that as a Stretch Goal and think about the outcome of the meeting being a Picture of Success. By a Picture of Success, I mean a compelling vision that aligns everybody's needs and priorities and describes what this organisation will look and feel like once you've solved all these challenges. Crack this and you've cracked your 'motivating without money' dilemma," suggests Richard.

Joe looks at Richard and the vision of the broken elastic band from last week's session enters his head.

"I'll think about it," he replies.

"Great!" Richard concludes, realising it is time to move Joe onto another subject.

"Going back to the last session, you mentioned an idea for a project with your kids. How's that going?" he asks.

"Well the idea was to combine some of my strengths to find a project that would create some happy memories for Harry and Amelia. You hit a nerve last week when you said being strong was not the same as being self-sufficient. It's a nerve my soon to be ex-wife has a habit of hitting too. So I've been thinking about what their strengths are, what they're good at that they enjoy doing.

"Harry is very creative. He loves making things look nice. Amelia is more interested in how things work than what they look like. This can lead to arguments. It probably hasn't helped that over the years I've tried to encourage them both to be good at everything, asking Harry to be more like Amelia and Amelia to be more like Harry. All they seem to do is bicker and compete for my attention. What they do have in common though, is a deep love for nature. So I came up with the idea of working together to set up our own little ecosystem in the form of a tropical fish tank. It plays to everyone's strengths, gives them an opportunity to learn about biology, maths, geography – and to be creative. It also means they'll finally have pets – something they've both been craving for years.

"Brilliant! And Lynette, what does she think?"

"Oh, the aquarium thing was kind of her idea. I'd been going down the line of joining them to the same gym as me but we got talking and came up with this idea, which we both think is much better.

"Anyway, we agreed a budget for the aquarium and I am going to introduce the idea to the kids this weekend. It's my turn to have them. That's if I have the energy," adds Joe. "There is so much going on at work that by the time it is the weekend I am exhausted. I consider it an achievement these days if I simply manage to keep them fed and stop them from killing each other."

"So, how can you top up your energy Joe? How can you use the sort of accelerators we use in business to energise you in your personal life? There will be such forces in your personal life too, things, people, activities that give you energy. For me they include spending time with my family and watching sport. What might be the equivalent for you Joe?" inquires Richard, aware that a lack of energy is a very real source of internal interference for Joe, which could become a performance risk if not dealt with intentionally.

"Well I used to go to the gym regularly. And years ago, before we had children, I ran a marathon. That was amazing. Even though I spent four hours every day training, I still had enough time and energy to do everything else. And the kids, spending time with them feels good – or it used to, before this ridiculous attention seeking behaviour started," admits Joe.

"So, how much time have you spent at the gym recently?" probes Richard.

"Almost none. I haven't been to the gym since Lynette and I separated," Joe replies, looking down at his feet. Bringing his gaze up, he leans back in his chair, staring thoughtfully across to the park where a group of children are playing. "Perhaps I need to get back into my regular workout routine," he adds tentatively.

"It's all about personal choice," Richard responds encouragingly. "It is clear to me that your energy at work is adversely impacted by a lack of exercise, but you will need to make a conscious effort to change the energy sapping routine you have established over the past year or so. You will need to be intentional. Are you ready to do this?" he pushes.

"I think so," replies Joe, wondering how on earth he is going to find the time. "I will update you next time we meet."

"And the next time we meet we'll review your progress against your Stretch Goals and take a look at how to deepen this new productive habit *Sharing Vision*, moving onto the next habit – *Sparking Engagement*. Then it's decision time. Will you be seeing more of me, or will it be our final session?" concludes Richard.

"I think you know the answer to that Richard. You can't leave me high and dry on the second habit. I need to know how to practise them all," Joe responds looking directly at Richard.

"Good. I'm pleased. Oh, and don't forget to fill in your Learning Journal!" Richard concludes, smiling and manoeuvring to shake Joe's hand.

Joe's Learning Journal Entry

1. I can overcome limiting weaknesses by dialling up my own strengths. I need to dial up my Strategic Mindedness strength far more over the coming weeks; this organisation needs a clear direction. I also need to dial up my Leading strength to build a more cohesive, collaborative team.

2. I've been focusing too much on task and results recently, at the expense of people and relationships. Some of my strengths are clearly in overdrive and putting this organisation's performance at risk! I need to call on some of my team's strengths to help here and profiling the team will help me to understand who can help where. At the same time, I need to intentionally build into my daily routine the habit of Developing Others.

3. There are several sources of interference putting my, and my team's, performance at risk. Creating and sharing a vision will help address some of the external sources of interference. My main internal source of interference is lack of personal energy. I am going to address this intentionally. I am committing to going back to the gym three times a week.

4. Breaking the news about the pay freeze is going to be tough. If I crack this Sharing Vision habit though, and involve the team in finding solutions and creating a longer term vision they can truly believe in, it may lessen the likely negative impact on morale and performance.

Chapter 4

Habit 2:
Sparking Engagement

**In which Joe practises optimising the strengths of
others and takes action to reduce performance risk...**

> **"Independence... [is] middle-class blasphemy.
> We are all dependent on one another, every soul
> of us on earth."**
> *G.B. Shaw, Pygmalion*

"So guys, there it is. My strengths, weaker areas and strengths in overdrive revealed; the issues this organisation is facing clarified; and an invitation for you all to identify your strengths and performance risks, using the Strengthscope360™ profiler.

"The goal of the next management meeting is to draw on our collective strengths to really nail a Picture of Success – by that I mean a compelling vision that aligns all our strengths and describes what this place is going to look like and what we want to achieve as a business," concludes Joe, pointing to the whiteboard on which he has just shared the challenges identified with Richard at his last session.

"Any questions?" he adds, wondering who is going to be the first person to point out the risks of ignoring weaknesses.

"Yes," pipes up Sally. "Why wait until the next management meeting to agree on what you call a Picture of Success? Why don't we all go complete this assessment now, have the meetings over the next three days and end the week with another meeting to keep momentum going?"

"Because we've got jobs to do," interjects Phil. "How is doing all this stuff going to help us close the gap we have between where we are now and where the business plan says we should be? It's nearly the end of the quarter. We need to make our numbers. If we have to do this development stuff, can't it wait until next quarter?"

Joe is shocked to hear the two voices he had been listening to in his head over the previous few weeks take on a life of their own in the boardroom, embodied in real people – his management team. The pros and the cons of focusing on strengths; the fear of not fixing problems and weaknesses first: it was fascinating listening to it all being played out before him. Hearing who said what gave him helpful clues as to what his team was made of, where different areas of strengths lay, who would choose the Path of Possibility™ and who would struggle. All was not what it seemed, he realised.

"OK guys, this is an interesting discussion. Sally, completing the assessments now *is* possible. The results will not be back before the end of the month though as we need to give colleagues the time to respond. Just as I invited you all to complete the assessment about me, you will be asked to nominate a number of colleagues to complete it about you. There's no reason why we can't end the week with a meeting about the vision though," suggests Joe.

"And Phil, understanding our individual and collective strengths is really going to help us to get our teams engaged and close the gap you're talking about. Once we know our strengths, stretching them takes very little extra time. We just purposefully embed practising new behaviours into our everyday lives. The type of behaviours I'm talking about include..." Joe moves over to the flip chart and bullets the following:

- *Finding new ways of performing current tasks that utilise our key strengths*

- *Getting involved in activities beyond our roles where we can make a positive difference using our strengths*
- *Helping and training others in our areas of strength*
- *Practising using our strengths in different situations.*

"Doing these sorts of things actually creates positive energy. It doesn't drain you at all. I know. I've been practising some of these. For example, I'm trying to use my *Initiative* strength now in this meeting, a strength I usually reserve for other forums. I'm finding that thinking and acting in this new strengths-focused way is helping me get through my 'to do' list quicker than ever before. I'm even finding time to go to the gym again," Joe explains.

"Isn't this just another way of saying 'do more with less' to an already overstretched team?" cuts in Raj.

"Well, that's one way to look at it. Some would say that 'do more with less' is the definition of innovation. I think most of our staff would like to be thought of as innovators. I guess the thing to point out is that Stretch is not about working harder. It's about working smarter, and that, if they're doing work that plays to their natural strengths, then they will feel more energised. I know I do."

Joe pauses. It seems as if everybody is listening. He decides to go one step further. Turning to the flip chart, he asks:

"What's the alternative?"

Drawing a line down the middle of the page, he labels one side 'Limitation' and the other 'Possibility'.

"As I see it, there are two alternatives. We can either keep on the Path of Limitation™, or move to the Path of Possibility™."

Leading a brainstorming session, he completes the sheet as follows.

LIMITATION	POSSIBILITY
Negative, uncooperative attitude	Positive 'can do' attitude
Bad morale	Engaged staff/ upbeat atmosphere
Poor customer service	Brilliant customer service
Silo thinking	Joined up thinking
Poor performance	Improved performance
Unwanted turnover	Talent retention
Lack of growth	Growth

"OK. I think I've done enough talking for one day. That's something else I want to change around here by the way. From now on, I want to contribute less to these meetings and for you all to contribute more. I can lead on the 'what' we need to achieve, but we all need to work out the 'how' together. There's one more thing I want to say though – well, ask, actually.

"I want to ask you all to go away and think about what it

would feel like if you were doing the best possible work that you could, that you were fully optimising your strengths. I want you to think about professional athletes and how they get better at what they do best. They take regular practice to stretch and build their physical and psychological strengths. I am offering you all the opportunity to do that here, to identify your areas of potential excellence and test your limits. I have research you can read, if you want, that shows that this approach works in business and that it will help us to overcome these issues, and to sustain progress.

"Now, a show of hands please, who wants to keep momentum going, as Sally suggested, and have the next meeting, the goal for which is to define our vision, or Picture of Success, on Friday and who wants to take another week. Hands up for Friday."

There are two hands in the air, belonging to Sally and Gwen. Raj and Phil's hands are firmly under the table. Both look defiant. After a long pause Mark sighs, "Well, we cannot let it be said there is a gender divide in this leadership team. It does make sense. We do need to do something. Why wait?" raising his hand above the table.

"Good. Raj and Phil, are you happy to give it a go, even though you're not 100% convinced? Your healthy scepticism will ensure balance. Shall we go for it?" leads Joe.

Raj and Phil agree to do so.

"OK then. Please find the time to complete your Strengthscope360™ assessments for tomorrow morning to get the ball rolling. I'll schedule individual meetings with you all for the end of the month with Richard, and with myself. We'll meet on Friday to nail the Picture of Success and look at how to get some quick wins," Joe concludes, before asking Raj and Phil to stay behind to discuss their concerns with him in more depth.

*

It is Thursday. Joe is updating Richard on the week's events.

"Well Joe. This is good news. You've made a great start. Once you've identified the strengths of your leadership team, you'll know better how to optimise them. This is a key behaviour associated with all the Stretch Leadership™ Habits. Even better news is that you're already practising some of the behaviours associated with the *Sparking Engagement* habit," reflects Richard.

"I am?" inquires Joe.

"You are. The behaviours associated with *Sparking Engagement* are: empowering people; encouraging openness (and being open to challenge); inspiring learning; and valuing feedback.

"Let's look at the first of these: empowering people. This involves sharing information and enabling people to decide how best to meet their own performance goals. It means delegating responsibility to staff throughout the organisation. Sounds like you've already set the scene for this to start happening with the leadership team," assesses Richard.

"Yes. So next I need to encourage them to pass it down the

line, I guess," Joe responds. He is feeling rather pleased with himself.

"Yes. How are you going to do this though? How can you motivate your staff to stretch and bring the power of their ideas into work?"

"I'm not sure. I suppose I need to get out of their way and just let them get on with things," ponders Joe.

"Exactly. You need to trust them and to show them that you trust them. This is the foundation of effective empowerment. You need to establish clear expectations and boundaries, then allow people to find their own path to their outcomes. This will enable them to take ownership of problems, solutions and results.

"If someone is new or inexperienced, you might need to give them more direction or guidance, but once they've gained experience, it's important to trust them and delegate responsibility, as well as more important tasks, to them. Without this level of trust and delegation, it will be tough to build a positive, innovative culture and you and the other members of the team won't be able to get on with the really important role of effectively leading Tiger towards its stretch goals," advises Richard.

"So, trust then?" summarises Joe, keen to move the session on.

"That's right. Onto the next behaviour then: encouraging openness. You told me that you were open to the challenges raised by team members at the last management meeting.

To truly engage the leadership team, and the wider team Joe, you need to be totally consistent. You need to create an open and respectful working environment where people feel like they can share their ideas and their views without criticism or judgement," Richard senses Joe's need for speed learning this session.

"OK. Surely a culture change like that will take forever though Richard? I don't know whether you've noticed, but I don't have a lot of time to play with here," Joe interjects.

"Well, you do have a wider team remember?" Richard responds.

"Soooo..." Joe drags the word out as if looking for an answer in the space between the consonant and the vowel. "Ah, I get it, I can give one of them a Stretch Goal to make this happen, maybe they can put in place practices and mechanisms to change the way we do things," he concludes.

"Good plan. How will you ensure that learning is always practised and becomes the way you do things around here then? How will you ensure that all staff have challenging opportunities that will help them grow?"

"Well, I guess I need a starting point. I need to understand all of their strengths, skills, aspirations and values in order to help them find challenging Stretch opportunities," Joe reflects.

"Go on," encourages Richard.

"And then I need to empower one of the leadership team to

make this culture change happen. It's another Stretch Project isn't it?" smiles Joe.

"See, you're already getting the hang of the first behaviour; you've just empowered two members of your team!" laughs Richard as he thinks, not for the first time that day, how much he loves his job.

"What are you going to do about the final behaviour, valuing feedback?" Richard probes.

"Well, it immediately springs to mind that we already practise this behaviour in various ways. Getting the leadership team to undertake the Strengthscope360™ exercise demonstrates we value feedback. Maybe we should extend it across the whole organisation.

"We also have a staff engagement survey and a customer feedback survey," Joe advises.

"Can you think of any other ways you can canvass opinions, or feedback?" Richard pushes.

"Well, I guess we could survey colleagues in our other offices around the world about their perception of our performance and culture in the region," Joe replies beginning to look distracted.

"Good. One other idea I've seen work is carrying out 'stay' interviews as well as the more traditional style 'exit' interviews. Finding out why key talent stays here and clarifying any of their concerns," Richard adds.

"I'll remember to try that, if any of our talent stays," Joe jokes, dryly.

Richard, recognising the giveaway sign of Joe's defensive use of humour, realises that Joe is in danger of stretching too far beyond his Comfort Zone, too quickly. He decides to round up the session.

"I look forward to hearing how the meeting goes tomorrow. Enjoy the rest of today because from tomorrow you're going to have to start turning the heat up. Once you've got these guys engaged, you need to start practising the third Stretch Leadership™ Habit – *Skilfully Executing*. This involves the behaviour of stretching people to their limits – but no further – and ensuring results get delivered. Something we'll discuss at our next session," Richard says rather purposefully as he navigates his way towards the door.

Joe returns to his desk and smiles as he sees an elastic band discarded on his desk. His smile fades as he realises that he has not spoken with Richard about breaking the news of the pay freeze. Remembering Richard's advice from the previous session, he relaxes a bit, deciding to fill in his Learning Journal whilst things are still fresh in his mind.

Joe's Learning Journal

1. Four key behaviours are associated with the Sparking Engagement habit: empowering people; encouraging openness; inspiring learning; and valuing feedback. It is crucial to optimise my own strengths and those of my colleagues too.

2. To embed all these behaviours, we need to create a culture where people feel valued, involved and trusted. I think Gwen will be brilliant at helping us to achieve this and I'm going to ask her if she'd like it as a Stretch Project. If she does, I'm going to offer to support her in creating and implementing a plan based on encouraging a highly motivating environment that ensures we are the sector's employer of choice, regardless of the pay freeze.

3. I'm confident that we're already doing a lot of this. We're just not letting people know we value it. I am going to make a conscious effort to notice where and when we are doing this everyday and to encourage and celebrate it. That will help to keep us on the Path of Possibility™.

Chapter 5

Habit 3:
Skilfully Executing

In which Joe practises stretching the limits and reinforces a culture of Positive Stretch...

"Start by doing what's necessary, then what's possible and suddenly you are doing the impossible."
Saint Francis of Assisi

It is Friday morning and Joe is intent on practising the new behaviours he has learned to help spark engagement. He thanks everybody for completing their Strengthscope360™ assessment and asks each for feedback about how they felt after completing the assessment. Most agree that it felt energising. Some admit that they are a little anxious about the feedback they'll be getting from the colleagues they'd invited to contribute.

"Tell me about it!" he laughs. "I'm still recovering from what you all said about me. In fact, let's not talk about it. Let's get cracking with crystallising our Picture of Success – what this organisation will look and feel like in, let's say one year's time, and what we will have achieved," he continues.

Working through an exercise Richard had shown him, Joe facilitates a discussion, with the help of post-it notes, culminating in the following succinct statement:

'Tiger created the future of recruitment.'

Working with the team to visualise and list what people would be saying about them when they had achieved this, what they would be doing, what other signs of success there would be to signify that they had achieved their goal, was like lighting a torch. Well, for most of the team.

"That was a brilliant session everybody, thanks for contributing so openly. Oh, and by the way, I was joking about your feedback being hard to swallow. I found it very enlightening and believe it's helping me to get my act together and become a better leader. I think you'll be surprised about how helpful the insights you give each other are too," Joe concludes.

"Joe. I need a word," Phil states flatly as the others head to the door.

Phil was the only member of the team who had not completed the Strengthscope360™ assessment. Observing Phil's contribution – or lack thereof – during this session, Joe knows what he has to do.

"Sure Phil, come this way," he responds calmly, leading Phil to his office.

An animated and open discussion about Phil's Comfort Zone begins. Phil lists too many reasons why he cannot move beyond his Comfort Zone. He questions the reality of a Zone of Stretch where peak performance happens, or the need for one. Focusing in on the Panic and Burnout Zone, he claims Joe's actions will push the entire team over the edge. He also emphasises the need for the team to get on with the 'day job' rather than being distracted by 'all this culture change and development stuff'.

Thirty minutes later, Phil emerges from Joe's office. The two have come to an agreement. While they concur that Phil has the right skills for the position, which is why he was recruited, his strengths and mindset do not lend themselves to easily adapting and thriving in the type of culture Tiger is encouraging. Phil enjoys the Comfort Zone and is simply not willing to do what is necessary to go beyond it, or even to expand it. He has always dreamed of setting up his own business, one that fitted in around his family and lifestyle. Joe hands him a lifeline – a day a week as financial advisor to Tiger Recruitment for a period of three months, with an opportunity to be introduced to other organisations in the Tiger network. Phil is, in his own quiet way, very pleased with the agreement he has struck with Joe. Joe is frankly relieved, especially as he is confident that he can draw on the strengths of his team to cover for Phil's absence until a permanent replacement is found.

*

"You have the makings of a very powerful team here Joe," reassures Richard as he concludes his summary of the management team's Strengthscope360™ profiles.

"Between you, your team inhabits every area of that strengths wheel we talked about, so you know you have the right mix of strengths to improve the performance of this business. The not so good news is that you lack a team member with *Developing Others* as a core strength. This may become a limiting weakness if you do not address it intentionally.

"The next step is to look at these people to see where they fall in the Passion-Performance Grid," advises Richard as he brings a graphic up on his computer screen.

Passion-Performance Grid

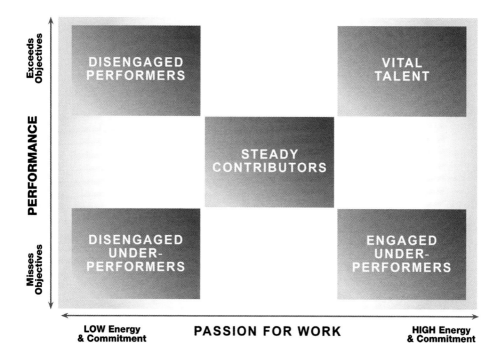

The clues given at the meeting earlier in the week, and the knowledge provided by the Strengthscope360™ profiles, make placing the management team members on this grid an easy task for Joe. The outcome though is a little disturbing. With Phil (who Joe had once thought of as his heir apparent) gone, Mark falling into the disengaged underperformer area and Raj fitting the engaged underperformer description, Joe suddenly feels anxious. Pulling himself back onto the Path of Possibility™, he notes that at least Gwen is a steady contributor and Sally is vital talent.

"How would it feel to have all members of your team sitting up there with Sally?" asks Richard.

"I have no idea, but if they were, I sure as hell wouldn't be sitting here having this conversation with you Richard!" jokes Joe.

"Do you think it is possible?" pushes Richard.

"I think it's unlikely, given recent performances but I'm guessing you're going to tell me that it is and that it's all about Stretch," replies Joe.

"Correct. By positively stretching each team member, aligning their strengths to their roles, setting appropriate Stretch Goals and Stretch Projects, there is no reason why your leadership team cannot all be contributing at the level that Sally is. The key is to set positive – not negative – Stretch challenges Joe.

"What do you think the difference is between Positive Stretch and Negative Stretch, Joe? How will you know if you're on the right track?" asks Richard.

"I guess Negative Stretch is asking them to change too quickly. There'll be signs that they are hurting," Joe responds, rubbing the back of his neck as he leans back in his chair.

"Kind of, but not quite. All Stretch hurts a bit to start off with. If it doesn't, it isn't Stretch. It's more about whether you're asking them to Stretch in areas of strength or not, and whether you're providing support.

"Positive Stretch is usually in line with the person's strengths and is supported. Negative Stretch is unsupported challenge in an area of non-strength or weakness. Like expecting a fish to swim out of water," concludes Richard.

"OK. So what do I need to do next then Richard?" asks Joe, picking up the pace.

"Well, you need to have some firm but supportive conversations with those guys and encourage them to set their own Stretch agendas, while you focus on staying on course with yours. One thing that will help you stay in Positive Stretch is to take a good look around at who you have to help you. The best leaders I've ever worked with have not just sought support from coaches. They've also informally appointed support from their personal and professional networks," replies Richard.

"What sort of support?" asks an intrigued Joe.

"Well, different types from different people. Typically they've turned to someone in a similar situation to themselves, with similar interests and goals to support them as a collaborator; to someone with strong interpersonal skills and networks as a connector; to someone strong on empathy and encouragement to provide emotional support, kind of like a counsellor; to someone strong on optimism for encouragement and to someone within the industry, steeped in experience, for long term support, guidance and wisdom, kind of like a mentor. It's like selecting your own personal board of directors[1] really," Richard explains.

[1] "Personal Board of Directors" is a term used by Clifton, D. And Nelson, P. (1992) in *Soar with Your Strengths*, New York: Dell Publishing.

"Shall we look at who might be on your board?"

Twenty minutes later, reviewing the strengths of those around him with Richard's help, Joe has written the following in his notebook:

Ahmed (colleague from a previous role) – Collaborator
Gwen – Connector
Lynette – Counsellor
Sally – Encourager
Kelly - Mentor

Joe is reeling with shock from the realisation that his estranged wife's strengths make her the perfect counsellor and that Kelly's strengths make her the perfect mentor. Strangely, he is more at ease with addressing the unfinished business relating to the management team's absence of vital talent, not to mention the *Developing Others* strength, than he is to asking these two for support.

"How are you feeling Joe?" asks Richard.

"Positively Stretched Richard! I'm very curious to find out what people's reactions are going to be to their profiles, and to what their suggestions are going to be around aligning their strengths to roles. Kind of like Sally yesterday, I'm just keen to keep up the momentum, to move from action to agility," Joe responds, remembering the expedition analogy Richard had shared with him in their first session.

"I'm also thinking that I should ask the rest of the team to form their own personal development boards too. I think it's a powerful way to help keep yourself on track, or can be if you have the right support around you," he adds.

"Good idea. Let's add that to the Strengthscope360™ review sessions we have with each of them then," concludes Richard, as he prepares for the first such meeting with Mark. "We could simultaneously introduce them to the first behaviour linked to the third habit of skilfully executing," suggests Richard.

"Which is?" enquires Joe.

"Setting clear, stretching and achievable performance expectations and ensuring people are held accountable to these," advises Richard.

"Well, I'm ahead of the curve here. I've already got that covered. What do I need to do next to be able to execute things skilfully?" asks a smiling Joe.

"Encourage the rest of your leadership team to adopt this behaviour and continue to take decisive action to deal with performance shortfalls and unproductive behaviour, just like you did with Phil. Encouraging the rest of the leadership team to do likewise too, of course," Richard responds quickly, recognising Joe's eagerness to learn as much as possible this session.

"OK," acknowledges Joe.

"Regularly reviewing progress to stay on track and maintain momentum is the third behaviour linked to skilfully executing. Inviting regular input from employees and other stakeholders and building this into decisions and plans is the final behaviour. Shall we get to it?" asks Richard, as he and Joe prepare to enter their first Strengthscope360™ feedback session with Mark.

*

It is the next management meeting. Each member of the team has met with Richard and with Joe to look in detail at how to optimise their strengths and reduce their performance risks. At these sessions, Joe had been sure to encourage the new behaviours he was himself still learning, setting each of them specific Stretch Goals. He had also taken some pretty decisive actions to deal with performance shortfalls within the team.

The team is about to find out...

"So, the good news is that we have a good spread of strengths and skills to help us get back on track. Perhaps you'd each like to share with us your feedback and plans?"

One by one, each member of the team shares their key strengths, observations about performance risks and plans about their Stretch Goals and Projects.

Things are going really well. Raj is to head a Stretch Project around networks. Gwen is to lead one looking into culture and talent. Having identified that a key member of her team, the HR manager Jane, has *Developing Others* as a strength, she is to share a lot of this work.

There comes a surprise though when it's Mark's turn.

"So, do you want to tell them or shall I?" asks Mark, looking at Sally.

"Go for it. I'll join in where I need to," Sally replies after a pregnant pause.

The tension is palpable. The team is still reeling with shock that Phil is no longer with them. They are wondering 'What now?'

"So guys. This is goodbye. It seems that I am not a natural operations director," he states solemnly.

Sally, following his lead, stands up too. She announces: "And it's goodbye from me also. Seems that I am not a natural sales and marketing director."

Raj and Gwen are stunned. They do not know where to look or what to say. They had been carried away by the positive wave of their own reviews and were just beginning to think that this stuff worked. They really had not expected this.

"But it's hello from me," interjects a playful Mark, "your new sales and marketing director."

"And it's hello from me too, your new operations director," laughs Sally.

Gwen and Raj are visibly relieved, Joe amused, as Mark goes on to explain.

"When I got my report it all became obvious. My top three strengths are *Relationship Building*, *Flexibility* and *Collaboration*. I'm really people focused. Reading that was one of those light bulb moments; I realised how much I missed using these strengths in a sales environment. I realised that I was frustrated in an operations role, which requires different strengths," Mark shares.

"And when I got my report, I realised that my top strengths, *Efficiency*, *Detail Orientation* and *Optimism* were not being given enough space to flourish. Although I do enjoy working with people, I'm very process driven and having sorted out all the processes in sales and marketing, I'm a little bored. When we had our one-to-ones with Richard and Joe, it soon became clear that there was an answer. A job swap!" interjects Sally.

"And I for one am delighted to be moving back to my natural habitat, sales and marketing. I'm in my element when networking and doing deals. Without jumping straight into strategy, I've a feeling the way to increase sales in the current environment is to drive new products through new partnership initiatives so that's my Stretch Project. I know how to do this. I've done it before. I want to do it and I know that Sally's extraordinary ability to spot detail and ensure follow-through will serve us all better if she takes the operations role," enthuses Mark.

"Yes!" laughs Sally. My *Efficiency* and *Detail Orientation* strengths will enable me to work with you all to realign our processes so we can get motoring sooner rather than later. My *Optimism* strength may be in what Joe calls 'overdrive' here but I'm really looking forward to this opportunity," she adds.

The team all congratulate each other, they are buoyant and raring to go. Joe decides to remind them of a few basics whilst the mood is right.

"So. Looks like we have a plan coming together. I just want to remind us all, including myself, of a few housekeeping items... rules if you like. Just because Gwen and Jane are leading on the culture project doesn't mean we can sit back and watch. Each and every one of us around this table needs to start building *Developing Others* into our daily routine. This is especially important as none of us have this as a natural strength. We need to be really intentional about it if things are going to change around here.

"From now on, we all know what we're accountable for and we all know what each other's natural strengths are. We know we can call on the strengths of each other, and those around us. The more we do this, the better we'll get at it.

"Let's remember, we are all here to help each other overcome our personal performance shortfalls, or energy blockers, and we're going to need to be, especially when we roll out the news about the pay freeze I shared with you each at our one-to-ones. The goal of the next management meeting is to decide how to communicate this to the rest of our teams in a way that will help them to accept it.

"Oh, and remember the personal development board idea we talked about at the one-to-ones? Please consider setting one up. I think it will really help us all," concludes Joe, who is really rather pleased with his team. He doesn't feel like he's lost a key member. He feels like he's found four.

Emboldened by his success, Joe decides to take the step of sharing with Kelly what he has been working on, and asking her to take on the role of mentor in his personal development board.

Having clearly defined what he wanted from her the night before, he prepares himself mentally before making the call. Whilst sharing the role of mentor and boss is not exactly textbook management technique, Joe reasons that it is leading beyond boundaries and that he has far more to gain than to lose from such an arrangement. He makes the call...

"Right Joe. I know I told you not to come to me with complaints about your team but I was not expecting this!

"It all sounds nice to do and I hear that it's getting some results but I'm not hearing enough yet. It sounds like this whole Stretch thing is just going to eat into time, not to mention money. If I'm going to invest in this I really need you to show me how this is going to turn us around and help us make the numbers," Kelly summarises. "And have you even told your staff about the pay freeze yet?" she adds, clearly irritated.

"Not yet Kelly. I've told the leadership team, but we've decided not to share the news more widely just yet. We want to give them something to believe in before we take away something they expect. Don't worry, we've got it covered. And we've ensured that this has not cost you anything to date Kelly. We have financed it from existing budgets. All I ask is for you to take on the role of being my mentor and help me to better understand the trends and innovations in the US recruitment market, so I can bring the best of it over here.

"And I don't think it is down to just me to show you how this is going to turn us around. Come over and meet the team. Each of them has a story to share. Each of them is achieving some quick wins that will demonstrate how we're going to do more than just make our numbers, pay freeze or no pay freeze," Joe replies, realising that he is actually enjoying this conversation.

"OK. I'll come. I'm making no promises Joe, but I will come and I will listen. And I will be happy to act as your mentor too," Kelly concludes.

Joe puts down the phone, leans back in his chair and looks out over the park. Smiling, he picks up his pen and journal and completes another entry.

Joe's Learning Journal Entry

1. People like clear leadership. Most people like to be Positively Stretched. Once you help them to understand what needs to be achieved and make them aware of their strengths and how to use them productively, they can work out the 'how' and will be more inspired to perform the job to a high standard.

2. We need to harness passion to drive performance so that every member of this team has the opportunity to achieve their full potential. The way to do this is to spot people's strengths and skills and actively develop talent and future leaders. We need to call on the individuals who have the best strengths for the task in hand and support each other to reduce areas of performance risk. I will take personal responsibility to review the finance team's talent pool and fill the finance director vacancy.

3. I need to ensure I stay, and keep the team, in Positive Stretch. The way to do this is to align goals to strengths and to continue to provide support.

4. Dealing swiftly with people whose values and attitudes don't match those of the organisation is really important.

5. Even though Kelly has not agreed to anything yet, other than to be my mentor, I feel really hopeful

that, through strong teamwork and application of our collective strengths, we can turn this business around and gain her support for our new vision, culture and Stretch Goals.

Chapter 6

Habit 3:

Skilfully Executing continued...

In which Joe continues to Stretch the limits...

"We are what we repeatedly do. Excellence, then, is not an act, but a habit."
Aristotle

"Yaaaay! Dad it's beautiful. When can we get the fish? Can we go get them now?" gushes Harry, stepping back to look at the tropical tank he has just set up with Amelia and his dad.

"What do you think Amelia?" prompts Joe who, for once, has noticed that his usually talkative daughter is actually being quiet.

"I really enjoyed setting that up but I'm a little worried that we've got it wrong and if we introduce fish, they'll just die – or eat each other," she explains.

"Well, what did the book say about when to introduce fish?" Joe asks.

"To leave it three to five days for the water to settle and the plants to do their stuff oxygenating the water, or something; then to test the water for levels of pH, chlorine and other chemicals. We can take a sample to the pet shop and they will run the tests. Then, if the temperature is stable too (Dad, you're going to have to keep checking the thermometer and make sure it stays within this green safety zone), we can add our first couple of fish," Amelia explains.

"And don't forget about the lights Dad. You need to switch the day-time light off and the night-time light on every evening, and the night-time light off and day-time light on every morning to help establish the cycle," adds Harry.

"Dad, can we come after school on Wednesday and go back to the pet shop with the water samples? PLEASE?" he urges.

"Yeah, can we?" pipes in Amelia.

"Well, if your mum says so, I don't see why not. Don't be too disappointed if the water isn't ready though. It may take more time, but we may as well go for it," Joe answers, delighted that his kids, for the first time in a while, are actually keen to see more of him.

"Come on, let's get you home, then we can ask. I need to talk to your mum about something else anyway," Joe adds, ushering them out of the apartment and into the car.

*

It is the next morning. Lynette accepted Joe's offer of the role as his counsellor on his new personal board of directors, having at first joked that she wanted to take legal advice. At least, he _thought_ she was joking. Now he is sitting with his coach, Richard, and is suddenly very conscious of how much he has changed in such a short period of time.

"Good. Now, let's look in more detail at how to practice the Stretch Habit of _Skilfully Executing_," Richard states, having reviewed developments against the targets from the previous session.

"You've already been exerting Positive Stretch, I can see that. It's a shame Phil is unwilling to move out of his Comfort Zone. I think the solution you arrived at though is good. It's also good that you agreed on the short, medium and long-term goals and that each leader is doing the same with their team. You really are leading beyond boundaries Joe. Let's try and capture where we are now for you, the leadership team and the wider organisation," Richard adds as they begin to map out Stretch Goals and success measures, identifying which strengths will enable each goal.

"This is all very well, Richard," sighs Joe, looking at the road map he and Richard have been creating half an hour later. "But how am I going to get some of those guys to keep up with me? Some of them are just not driven. Some of them avoid making decisions at all costs. Plus, Gwen tells me there is a perception that Phil got fired for challenging my authority, which is just not true. But if that is what people believe, they're hardly going to start making decisions for themselves are they?"

"Brilliant!" Richard responds, leaning forward and smiling.

"Pardon?" Joe asks, after a short pause, leaning back, frowning.

"This is brilliant. You have recognised that you are edging out of your Zone of Stretch and Peak Performance before you have gone so far as to dip your toe in the Panic and Burnout Zone. This is an important skill for leaders. Well done!" Richard congratulates Joe.

Joe remains silent, looking at Richard for clues.

"What's the best thing you can do now?" prompts Richard.

"Not panic?" suggests Joe, picking up on Richard's mention of the Panic and Burnout Zone.

"What else?"

"I don't get it," states a frustrated, tired and distracted Joe.

"Let's go back a bit to explore Stretch in more detail," Richard pulls up the Stretch Zone slide, which suddenly reminds Joe of a darts board, a game he has never had much patience for.

The Stretch Zone

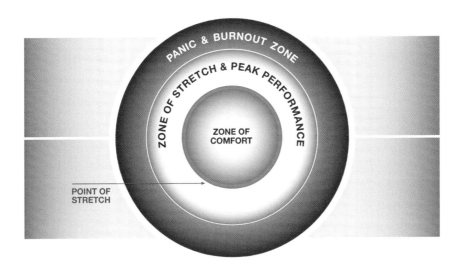

"When you are here," Richard points to the centre, labelled Zone of Comfort, "what are you doing, exactly, and what does it feel like?"

"Well, I'm focusing on tasks, in control, doing things, achieving goals, with others following me. It feels easy – or at least it did when this approach was actually achieving goals."

"And, when you are here?" Richard points to the Zone of Stretch and Peak Performance.

"Well, I guess that's where I've been the last few weeks. Building strong teams, motivating people, delegating tasks and responsibilities. It's been working. We're already getting results and it feels more energising. It's created a lot more choices for us, when we were feeling trapped. It's made me, and this organisation as a whole, I think, feel more... powerful, I guess."

"So bring me back to that discussion you had with Phil in this room, when he questioned this approach, and your authority. Where in this model were you then?" pushes Richard.

"Here," Joe points to the Panic and Burnout Zone. He is beginning to question his decision about Phil, who, since the new arrangement, has actually been far more proactive and positive. He is wondering whether he made an overly rash decision and could have avoided taking such drastic action by looking for other ways to align Phil's strengths with his role.

"Were you? Or were you here?" Richard asks, pointing to the Point of Stretch.

"Ah. I get it! You're right. I created a choice, out of nowhere, when we were both feeling trapped, and it's working, even though people don't yet know it's working. Changing Phil's role from internal leader to external advisor engaged him. If things had stayed the same he'd have never engaged. He may have the right strengths for the role, but his values are not aligned with the new culture here. I've found a natural replacement for him within the finance team too. So, we have everything we need to move forward."

"Good. So, where are you now?"

"I'm here," Joe points to the edge between the Zone of Stretch and Peak Performance and the Panic and Burnout Zone.

"And where do you want to be?"

"Back here," Joe points to the Point of Stretch again.

"And how are you going to get there?" prompts Richard.

Joe stares blankly.

Richard pulls up his Path of Possibility™, as if to nudge Joe.

The Path of Possibility™

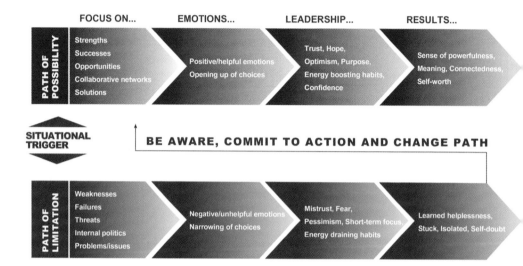

"Ah. I need to take the Path of Possibility™, not the Path of Limitation™. I need to focus on strengths, successes, opportunities, solutions and networks. Not on weaknesses, failures, threats and all that stuff," Joe reels off, sounding, looking and feeling more buoyant.

"And, if you continue to navigate along that path, what will happen to the atmosphere here, the culture of this place?" Richard pushes.

"Well, I'll be more predictable and people will begin to trust me. We'll all be more optimistic. We'll share a sense of purpose. We'll all pick up your energy boosting habits and before we know it we'll all be setting off on another expedition – together."

"Good. Back to your road map then. You state your Personal Stretch Goals as: strengthening your leadership, particularly your ability to engage and motivate team members; and improving your work life balance. Your Personal Success Measures (how you will know when you achieve your goals) are: you'll be getting positive feedback from Kelly and the leadership team; and you'll be leaving work on time at least once a week. Which of your Significant Seven strengths will enable you to achieve these goals?"

"*Leading*, *Strategic Mindedness* and *Initiative*?" suggests Joe.

"Good, and your Team Stretch Goal is: to ensure effective teamwork and positive engagement of each team member. Your Team Success Measures are: you'll be retaining key team members and delivering the vision and strategic plan. And the staff morale will have increased (you'll know this as it will be reflected in the staff survey as well as their general behaviour, attitude and mood). Which strengths are going to help you here?"

"*Leading*, *Results Focus* and *Common Sense*," Joe states this time, rather than suggests.

"OK. Now you've got the hang of it, why don't you look at Organisational Stretch Goals with the team? Get them to develop road maps for their teams too. If this team is to commit to your road map they need to feel like it's theirs, like they were involved in creating it. Also, take time to look at this road map again when I'm gone and think about which members of your personal development board, or your leadership team, can help you and where. Think about the strengths they have and where you can dial them up. Any questions?" asks Richard.

"Yes, actually," Joe responds slowly, formulating the question in his mind as he is speaking.

"You managed to bring me back to the Path of Possibility™ pretty quickly there. You made it look easy. I'm not yet good enough at this balancing act to do this. Can you help me recognise when I'm tipping over (or members of my team are) and how to help?"

"Sure. It's all about 'Flow', Joe. In order to achieve Flow, people need to have a passion and a desire to do the job in hand. They need to feel strengthened by it. There also needs to be a good match between the level of skills required to complete the task, and the level of challenge and Stretch the task provides. If there is no Stretch, they are likely to quickly lose interest, become disengaged, and their performance and effort will weaken.

"Too much Stretch and the reverse is true. They feel incompetent, frustrated, and their performance is adversely impacted too.

"The trick is to find the degree of Stretch people are currently feeling, then to cooperatively create new challenges or goals that make them feel challenged and engaged, but not overwhelmed. This is exactly what you did with Phil, Mark and Sally. Well done!

"Calibrating personal, team and organisational strengths in this way keeps confidence, commitment and contribution high and we've just gone through the blueprint – this road map – to execute this.

"The main thing to remember in all of this Joe, is not to criticise yourself when you do start to feel the Stretch. Feeling it means it's working Joe. Don't forget, you're trying to break habits and behaviours you've been living for years as well as learning new ones." Richard brings up on screen the Stretch Leadership™ Model he had introduced Joe to in their first session.

Stretch Leadership™ Model

"Just because you now have this knowledge, doesn't mean that changing the products of nature and nurture is going to come easily. You are still new to this way of leading, so be easy on yourself Joe," Richard continues.

"The key is to recognise when you are edging towards the Panic & Burnout Zone. Observe yourself for about a week and make a note of how it feels when you are in the Panic Zone. What are some of the things you feel? What do you see yourself doing? What do you hear yourself saying? What do you see others doing and others saying?

"For example, I know when I am in the Panic Zone because I feel a determination to make sure everyone knows I feel fine. So if someone asks how I am I say 'Fine. I'm fine. I'm fine'. I tend to repeat the word and want to move on and not talk about my feelings. Then on reflection I think back and realise I wasn't 'fine'. I just didn't know how to say what I was feeling or didn't feel able to say it to that person.

"A former colleague pointed out to me that this was a warning sign. You'll have similar warning signs people can make you aware of. Like rolling up your sleeves, for example," Richard smiles, watching Joe roll up his sleeves.

"Great leaders have enough humility to open themselves up and allow others in. Many actually share their triggers with those close to them and ask them to point out to them if they spot any warning signs," he concludes.

Joe is not sure what to say. He had never realised he wore his anxiety, literally, on his shirt sleeves and his former self is not at all comfortable with the idea of sharing with people that he is not actually always in control.

He thanks Richard, choosing to mull over his advice. He has other things to deal with first, like catching up on progress with the various Stretch Projects and working out how to communicate the pay freeze with the wider team. Kelly is coming across for the next management meeting so he really wants to make sure the new way of working is working.

*

It is the next management meeting. Everybody has presented their team's progress against Stretch Goals, apart from Gwen. It is her turn. She is aware how directly her team's work will feed into the next item on the agenda, sharing the news about the pay freeze. She seems quite calm:

"So we've accelerated the Strengthscope360™ profiling and each of us will have one-to-one meetings with our staff, agreeing personal development and other Stretch Goals. We've set up regular staff briefings and we've all started to make ourselves more visible within our teams – I think textbooks call it 'Management By Walking About' or something. We're all going to take our key team members to lunch once a month and we've invited the wider team to suggest other ways to encourage us to all interact with each other outside of meetings," Gwen advises.

"I'm also recommending we put ourselves and all our managers on the strengths coaching programme Richard told us about in our feedback sessions, and look for ways to set up peer mentoring (once we've done our talent reviews that is)," she continues.

"The cross-department 'lunch and learn' sessions you introduced are going really well Gwen," Mark pitches in. "One result of the last one was that we identified and invited some of our key customers to participate in designing and trialling some of our new online offerings," he concludes.

"So, if we're about to have one-to-one performance reviews in this new format, hadn't we best come up with a strategy for telling them about the pay freeze?" asks Sally. "I mean, how do you think they're going to take the news?" she adds.

"Well, they will all react differently. I think we can lessen the negative impact and get them to accept it if we work on this together, agree how to communicate it in a way that helps them understand that this is a temporary situation. We need to help them believe that they can shape their own future to ensure that this doesn't need to last longer than this quarter," Gwen advises.

"I agree. And I've been looking into it and it seems that we're not the only ones in this boat. Many of our competitors are laying people off as well as putting a freeze on bonuses and commissions, so if they're not happy and decide to go elsewhere, they'll soon realise they've got the best deal here, thanks to all these other initiatives we're working on," Raj interjects.

"Let's brainstorm some low cost ways to motivate people," Sally says, walking over to the flip chart.

Twenty minutes later they have a set of bullets that she takes away as input into a reward and recognition programme, something they will all use during their team meetings and one-to-ones with staff.

Ways to motivate without money

1.   Private notes of congratulations
2.   Public recognition at all staff meetings
3.   Time off for personal development or charity work
4.   Free/subsidised lunches
5.   Games room
6.   Team rewards/activity days
7.   Short breaks for top performers

Joe leaves the meeting relaxed. He decides to take ten minutes to crystallise his learning and the team's progress before leaving on time to make it to the gym before picking up the kids.

Joe's Learning Journal Entry

What a week! Thought I'd summarise progress as well as learning today.

1. The behaviours relating to the Skilfully Executing habit are self starting. We're setting clear, stretching and achievable performance expectations and ensuring people are held accountable to these. We're anticipating and taking decisive action to deal with performance shortfalls and unproductive behaviour. We're regularly reviewing progress to stay on track and maintain momentum. And we're inviting regular input from employees/stakeholders and building it into our decisions and plans.

2. Gwen is well ahead on her Stretch Project, creating an environment that encourages Stretch and experimentation. Seems that developing others was a hidden strength for Gwen. Working alongside Jane is really helping too. They're becoming quite a double act!

3. Sally is simplifying and streamlining our reward and recognition process to ensure everyone is provided with positive recognition and feedback and to help us break the news about the pay freeze.

4. We've created an environment of Positive Stretch. People are moving beyond their Comfort Zone. Cross discipline teams are working on new product ideas.

Some of our staff are working on projects with our key clients, helping them to formulate their recruitment strategies whilst finding out what they actually need in this new economic environment. Our leadership team is offering mentoring to students studying business studies at a local college and several of us are thinking about Stretch Projects outside of work too.

5. Mark's been leading a team on a Stretch Project that has identified a great new product opportunity. We've handed over the findings to Sally, who is leading a team looking into how we can bring it to market before the end of the year. She is presenting the findings at the next management meeting, at which Kelly will be present. Sally and Mark are very excited about it, and their moods seem to be infecting the rest of the team. Let's hope Kelly gets it.

Chapter 7

Habit 4:
Sustaining Progress

In which Joe recognises achievement...

"Practice isn't the thing you do once you're good. It's the thing you do that makes you good."
Malcolm Gladwell,
Blink: The Power of Thinking Without Thinking

It is the end of January. Tiger Online Recruitment is four months into its Stretch Programme. The short term goals set at the beginning of the period have been achieved. Processes are in place, driving the team towards achieving the longer-term goals. Joe is summarising the outcome of the latest activity in the leadership team's weekly meeting, and leading an exercise to complete the organisational road map.

Kelly is present and unusually silent.

"So, we are all agreed: our Organisational Stretch Goals to achieve by the end of the financial year are: strong growth in sales revenue; improvements in margins; recognition as market leader; launching the upgraded Career Toolkit for candidates (which was identified as a way forward by Mark's team in their Stretch Project – well done Mark's team); and achieving outstanding client retention and engagement during the period.

"Our Organisational Success Measures, how we know we've achieved our goals, are: we will have 100% growth in revenues with more than 15% margin; we will have won 15 new FTSE 100 clients; the Career Toolkit will be launched before the new financial year; and our client retention rates will have increased by 85% (with us having a host of positive testimonials to share off the back of our annual client survey).

"We have talked about how each of our individual strengths will enable us to achieve this, when some of us may need to dial down our strengths – such as me and my *Decisiveness* strength (I know you are all taking increased ownership for leading your areas now and I need to back off sometimes); and when we can call on others' strengths to help. For example, I can, and indeed will, call on Raj's *Efficiency* strength to ensure we are following through if I see this stuff isn't happening fast enough."

"I think this team is doing an amazing job driving the UK arm of Tiger Recruitment towards making our vision a reality. It really does feel to me like we're re-writing the recruitment industry handbook; creating the future; moving beyond boundaries. Agree?" asks Joe.

There is a chorus of affirmations from around the table, with one exception, Kelly, who remains thoughtfully silent.

"So, to that temporary sacrifice we've been talking about – the pay freeze. How has the news of that gone down?" he asks nobody in particular, all the time watching Kelly closely for any clues about what she is thinking.

"Well, nobody welcomed it with open arms but since we have ways other than pay to reward performance here now, it wasn't such a hard sell," Arthur, the recently appointed acting head of finance, advises.

"Even my team took it on the chin," Mark adds. "I don't know about the rest of you but the fire I feel in my gut since we've been on this Stretch Journey is reward enough for me. Getting them all to buy into our 'creating the future of the recruitment industry' vision was the first step I think. Once they got that, and saw examples of our new reward and recognition structure in action, they took it much better than I'd expected. They were very grateful we took the time to explain and listen. They're not happy but I think we're OK," Mark summarises.

Everyone around the table agrees with the exception of the still thoughtfully silent Kelly, silent apart from the sound of her pen jotting notes, that is.

"So, now over to Sally, who is going to lead us through an exercise exploring how we can build on our successes to help us achieve all this, doing more with less, if you like," Joe concludes.

Sally methodically and cheerfully facilitates a discussion that reviews the skills, wisdom and learning available in-house that will enable them to launch the new Career Toolkit. Widening the discussion out, she guides the team into describing the ways in which the change in mindset, culture, and indeed behaviour, have enabled them to come this far. Going further, they identify how this will enable them to expand out to the next level and deliver the first iPhone-compatible Career Toolkit in the marketplace. Mark contributes by describing the market opportunity, backing his claims up with research and statistics collected as part of the Stretch Project he led. He concludes by explaining how the new product will go viral if the team get it right and draw on the power of their collective strengths and networks.

"And make no mistake, our network is already growing. We've already recruited twelve partners from the outplacement sector to help us market this. It is what everyone is crying out for. Everyone stands to win. If we get this right, are first to market, and it has the quality hallmark we are known for running right through it, then, well, let's just say, we're going to have one monster of a kick off party at the beginning of the next financial year!"

Joe sits back and watches his team perform. They'd only been practising this approach for a few months and he'd seen individuals, and the team, shift mindset and behaviour significantly. Yet, while he had been keeping to his Stretch Goal and leaving work on time at least once a week, he knew that some of the people around the table had picked up his old habit of staying late, often burning the midnight oil.

'Still, at least they're practising the new habits too,' he reflects as the meeting, and the working day, draws to a close and a thoughtful Kelly leaves for the airport.

*

"I'm so sorry. Your water levels are not right yet. The pH, ammonia and saline levels are fine but the nitrates are high. Nitrates are toxic to fish so we need to get them down before you can introduce any," explains the sales assistant at the pet shop.

Joe sees Harry holding back tears. Before he can intervene, Amelia steps in.

"How toxic? And to which fish? Surely there are some fish, somewhere in the world, that live in nitrate-rich environments?"

"I like the way you're thinking," laughs the sales assistant, "you're probably right, but even if we could select them you'd be making your job going forward very difficult. You see, successful fish-keeping is all about managing the environment. Get that right and the fish flourish. It should be called water-keeping really, not fish-keeping."

Joe smiles, as he realises the same is true in the corporate world. Putting his hand on Harry's shoulder, he smiles at Amelia, and asks: "So, what can we do to get the nitrate levels down, and how long will it take?"

"Well, a partial water change of 20 %, putting the prescribed amount of this solution in will kick start your filter into converting the nitrate back into free nitrogen gas. You can also select some aquarium plants to help with the job," the assistant advises.

"Well get to it then Harry, go pick a plant – at least we'll be putting something alive in the tank when we get home. And Amelia, how about you take that solution and start to work out how much we need to add to a 48 litre tank? Meanwhile, I'll do what I'm best at. I'll pay."

They leave the shop subdued but hopeful.

"So kids, ready to give Mum a lesson on water-keeping?" Joe asks as they drive home, already preparing in his mind for his session with Richard the next day.

*

"So we reach the final Stretch Leadership™ Habit today Joe, *Sustaining Success*. Now, the way this works is that by picking up the other habits, you almost start practising this one automatically. I suggest I describe the behaviours associated with the habit and we consider whether you're already living them. Ready?" asks Richard.

"Ready," answers Joe.

"So, the first behaviour is challenging people to think and act in new and innovative ways," continues Richard.

"Tick," laughs Joe. "By simply identifying and sticking with the Stretch Projects and Stretch Goals, we are collectively practising that behaviour. Next!"

"Creating a safe environment that encourages considered risk taking and continuous improvement," laughs Richard.

"Tick. One of Gwen's Stretch Projects tackled this. Sally and Mark's role swaps are proof of risk taking and the way their new roles are panning out are delivering continuous improvements. Next!"

"Promoting a working environment which values experimentation and a commitment to learning," prompts Richard.

"Isn't that the same as the last one? Experimentation? Risk taking? Are they not the same thing?"

"Not necessarily and don't forget about 'valuing a commitment to learning'. How are you demonstrating that at the moment?" clarifies Richard.

"Well, I've – sorry 'we've' – introduced pilot projects to

incubate and test out new, innovative ideas, to see what we can learn from our partners. We're encouraging questions, challenge and inquiry at all our meetings. We're reviewing competitors' work and progress and trying to learn from their experiences – what's worked well and what has not. We're engaging customers in brainstorming forums and project teams to help design and/or improve products and services," lists Joe, delighted with himself as the answers stream into his consciousness.

"Gosh, quite a lot actually. I wonder what else we could be doing if we actually addressed the question directly, what was it again? Something like 'What can we do to promote a working environment which values experimentation and a commitment to learning?' wasn't it?" he adds, his thoughts really racing now.

"Yes, exactly that," interjects an amused Richard. He's always loved this session on the final habit.

"Well, I guess we could send the management team on study visits to other companies and our other offices worldwide to review practices, raise questions and gather ideas.

"We could review better practices in other sectors to see whether there are any ideas that can be incorporated, rather than reinventing the wheel. Companies like Facebook, Amazon, and Innocent could be good places to look for better practices I reckon," Joe is really on a roll now.

"You see the thing with those organisations is that they really encourage what the management books call 'intrapreneurship' don't they? I think that would work here.

"Crikey, Richard, I could go on forever. I wonder what you've seen working though? What do you think I should be doing differently?" asks Joe.

"I don't think you should be doing anything differently. Just keep doing more of the same," laughs Richard.

"Oh come on Richard, you can do better than that! Give me some ideas. What have you seen that works?" Joe is really enjoying this exchange. So is Richard.

"Well, you're already doing most of it. Managers and functional heads spending time going to team meetings of other functional areas to provide input and learn new ideas; thorough project reviews at the end of every project to analyse learning, including reasons for successes and failure. That sort of thing.

"One thing I've seen work really well is actively encouraging employees to spend work time pondering complex challenges and ways to solve them. Some companies, like 3M for example, set aside specific time to enable employees to come up with and refine new ideas for product and process innovation. They also ensure their senior management team take responsibility to personally sponsor key ideas and projects to increase their likelihood of success.

"Enough?" asks Richard, amused that he and Joe seem to be swapping roles.

"Yes, for now," laughs Joe, picking up the game. "Any more behaviours I need to practice?"

"Yes. The last behaviour associated with the *Sustaining Success* habit is recognising outstanding effort and celebrating achievement (even those small wins like completing a project on time) in a fair and appropriate way.

"Talking of which, I must congratulate you on quite a spectacular fortnight since we last met. You really are progressing. You must recognise that?" finishes Richard, aware that time has marched on even faster than usual in his sessions with Joe. "Want to share your learning?"

"Well, inspired by your talent for creating analogies, I think I may have come up with one of my own," Joe smiles.

"Go on..." Richard prompts, intrigued.

"Leadership is a lot like keeping fish. First of all you have to manage the environment and set everything in place to ensure the fish can each do their job properly. It's about water-keeping to start with, not fish-keeping.

"Then you have to select the right fish to live in the environment you've created. Just like you need a community of fish that work together to maintain the environment you've created – so algae eaters, bottom feeders, and fast fish that create water movement – so too do you need to select people with complementary strengths to maintain the corporate environment, and to keep things moving.

"And just like you can find natural solutions to put things right when they go wrong in the fish tank, so you can in the corporate world. But, just like in a fish tank, if you forget to monitor and support progress, things can start to go wrong. It's not just about setting Stretch Goals at the beginning of a project. It's about proactively monitoring and reviewing them throughout. That is how you maintain a Stretch Culture."

"Great analogy!" enthuses Richard. "Love the bit about keeping water not fish! Think I'll be borrowing that. I read recently that the water cycle is the most important natural phenomenon on Earth. It regulates our weather and the growth of food. It has no starting and no ending point but is a continuing process. So is your learning journey as a leader. I hear you're about to complete your first circuit with an away day style kick off party for the new financial year – further evidence that you're embedding these behaviours in your way of operating now. I know this because Kelly called me after your management meeting and asked to meet me before she flew back. We discussed taking this Positive Stretch approach across the other side of the pond. Evidence Joe, should you need it, that you've met your Stretch Goal.

"Anyway, this event is the perfect forum for you to introduce that final behaviour associated with the final Stretch Leadership™ Habit of *Sustaining Progress*; celebrating success," concludes Richard, with total confidence that Joe knows what to do next...

Joe's Learning Journal Entry

This stuff works!

Chapter 8

Postscript

**In which Joe celebrates success
and passes on his learning...**

"Celebrate what you want to see more of."
Thomas J. Peters

It had taken Gwen and her Stretch Team some doing to pull off the biggest celebration the company had ever hosted at such short notice, but a phone call from Kelly offering some budget and her support had been the only incentive they'd needed.

The Europe region had achieved all of its Stretch Goals. Following the Stretch Leadership™ Habits, they had achieved unprecedented growth in profit and overcome the short-term pay freeze. They had a clear strategy and sense of purpose. They had achieved the highest levels of job satisfaction amongst the people employed in any Tiger regional office, anywhere in the world. All this, and they had simplified and clarified their processes, ensuring they could be easily cascaded throughout the organisation.

In his end of year address, Joe revisited the vision they had developed and shared back in the Summer: *'Tiger created the future of recruitment'*. He explained how the region had come full circle and would be continuing its Stretch Journey by revisiting aspirations in the new financial year. He then showed a short film Gwen and Jane had helped him to secretly produce. The film celebrated the strengths and achievements of each member of the leadership team, and the members of their teams who had contributed to this success.

Joe was not the only leader to spring a surprise though. Kelly made an unexpected appearance presenting the TERET with the prestigious 'Tiger Team of the Year' award. She also announced that the team would be losing a leader in January. Gwen was to be seconded to the US office to lead a Stretch Project there. Jane would be stepping up to take the position of director of human resource in the UK.

Joe and the rest of the team were delighted for Gwen and their US colleagues. They knew, beyond doubt, that rigid boundaries and missed targets were a thing of the past because Tiger Online Recruitment was well and truly on the Path of Possibility™.

P.S. On starting her secondment, Gwen asked Joe to provide her with his top tips for leading at full Stretch. Below is his response...

My 7 Stretch Leadership™ Lessons

1.   Understand your strengths (what you're good at that gives you energy). Align them with your values, aspirations and abilities. Gain the Leadership Edge.

2.   Adopt the four Stretch Leadership™ Habits: Sharing Vision; Sparking Engagement; Skilfully Executing and Sustaining Progress. Positively Stretch your own strengths, those of your team and those of your organisation. Gain the Market Edge.

3.   Create a Road Map detailing Stretch Goals, Success Measures and Enabling Strengths. Ensure you and your team are aligned with these goals and that everybody's strengths are contributing to defined business outcomes.

4.   Recruit across the full spectrum of strengths. Align people's strengths with their roles and give them a clear vision – a reason to be passionate about their work. Inspire high performance. Provide encouragement and support.

5.   Choose the Path of Possibility™. The Path of Limitation™ is unproductive and drains your emotional, mental and physical energy. The Path of Possibility™

gives a sense of positive power and enhances productive energy. It gives staff a sense of meaning and connection. It helps ensure that targets are met, again and again.

6. Focus on strengths whilst addressing performance risks caused by limiting weaknesses, strengths in overdrive and sources of interference. Moderate the volume of your own strengths and call on the strengths of others when facing these risks. Just be disciplined about the stuff that doesn't energise you but that you know needs to be done. Focus on the benefits of doing these less savoury parts of your job to ensure risks don't derail you.

7. Stretch is a continuous journey. It revolves around the stages of aspiration, awareness, action, agility and achievement. Choose to take this journey. Stretch creates positive energy. Stretch sustains success.

Free Tools to Help Transform Your Leadership

For free downloadable resources and tools to help Stretch yourself, your team and your organisation, go to:

www.stretchleadership.com

Simply enter your details and the password **stretchleader** in the registration area provided to download your complementary resources and tools.

You will also be offered a 25% discount voucher on the Strengthscope360™ assessment and a telephone or one-to-one coaching session to help you optimise your strengths, reduce risk areas and put a leadership Stretch plan together to accelerate your effectiveness and results.

Strengthscope360™ is a world leading assessment profiler that provides a comprehensive measurement of an individual's strengths at work. It is used by leading organisations around the world and helps people understand:

- *Their standout strengths*
- *The performance risks that may arise when strengths go into overdrive*
- *The extent to which they are able to productively apply their strengths at work*
- *How visible their strengths are to others*
- *Recommendations to use their strengths more effectively and reduce areas of risk.*

About the Authors

James Brook, BA (Hons), MSocSc (Organisational Psychology), MBA, FCIPD
James is co-founder and Director of Strengths Partnership. He has around 20 years' experience in leadership development, organisational change and talent management, having worked in consulting and corporate roles internationally. Recent clients have included Facebook, ING Direct, Novartis Pharmaceuticals, Photobox, Takeda Pharmaceuticals, GSK and Tesco.

James is a regular speaker on strengths-focused leadership and talent development and has contributed a wide range of business and professional publications in the area. He has a Masters Degree in Industrial & Organisational Psychology, a MBA and is a Fellow of the CIPD.

Dr Paul Brewerton, BA (Hons), MA, MSc, PhD, Chartered Occupational Psychologist
Paul is co-founder and Director of Strengths Partnership. Paul is a Chartered Occupational Psychologist and Doctorate in Organisational Psychology with around 20 years' experience in individual, team and organisational development. Paul has worked across a wide variety of sectors; recent clients include Takeda, Tesco, Bank of England, Legal and General, Panasonic, Santander, Oracle, Royal Air Force and many more.

In recent years, Paul has dedicated his business activities to helping organisations translate a strengths-focused approach to bottom line business performance. He is a frequent contributor to business publications and regular conference speaker.

Strengths Partnership Ltd

Strengths Partnership (www.strengthspartnership.com) is a world leader in providing pragmatic strengths-based solutions to translate individual, team and organisational strengths into measurable success, innovation and engagement.

The company has five consulting practice areas: selection and assessment; leadership and talent development; coaching; building peak performing teams; and organisational development and effectiveness.

Strengths Partnership's Strengthscope™ strengths assessment suite is the most comprehensive on offer and has multiple applications across the full employee lifecycle.